10 CDS FOR A PENNY GROWING UP GEN X
WITH BRUISES, BURNT POP-TARTS, AND
ZERO THERAPY

10 CDs for a Penny Growing Up Gen X with Bruises, Burnt Pop-Tarts, and Zero Therapy

SERGIO SERNA

Joker &
the Queen
PUBLISHING

CONTENTS

Dedication - viii

~ ~

EPIGRAPH and Warning Label
1

~ 1 ~

Latchkey Nation
3

~ 2 ~

I Want My MTV
14

~ 3 ~

Style Wars
21

~ 4 ~

We Ate Like We Had a Death Wish
34

~ ~

Our Real Parents Were Television & Trauma
49

~5~

TV and Gen X
51

~~

Intermission: The Hormonal Truth
104

~6~

Playground Darwinism
110

~7~

Our Toys Could Kill You
130

~8~

We Were Internet Beta Testers
144

~9~

Gen X: The Movie
153

~10~

The Mall Was Our Internet
166

~11~

Gen X: We Came, We Saw, We Got PTSD
181

~12~

Burnt Pop-Tarts and Other Life Lessons
190

Acknowledgements - 197
About the Author - 199

To Patsy and Lindsay—my day ones before day ones were even a thing.

We weren't the damn Brady Bunch. Hell, we couldn't even get through breakfast without someone throwing shade or cereal. But through every fight, every laugh, every late-night couch confessional, and every tag-team mission, we were solid. Always.

Patsy, you really jumped a girl at lunch just for running her mouth about me. That's some next-level sister shit. Lindsay, your smart-ass comments cut deeper than grandma's chancla, but they always made me better.

I got lucky. I didn't just get sisters—I got bodyguards, roast masters, secret-keepers, and forever hype women. I love you both with everything I got, even when y'all drive me nuts.

You made me who I am. And I'm proud as hell to be your brother.

Joker and the Queen Publishing
243 E. Latimer Ave #3
Campbell, CA 95008

Cover design by Sergio Serna
Printed in the United States of America

First Edition: 2025
ISBN: 979-8-9992221-4-5

For all the latchkey kids who learned to survive before they ever learned to feel.....We made it. Sort of.

EPIGRAPH AND WARNING LABEL

"Our childhood was a social experiment with no control group and zero follow-up. The results? Sarcasm, grit, and deep trust issues."

— Sergio Serna

WARNING LABEL
(aka: Read This Before You Catch Feelings)
This book contains:

- *Language your parents used when they thought you were asleep*

- *Stories that might hit too close to home*

- *Mentions of broken toys, broken homes, and broken rules*

- *An absurd amount of Pop-Tarts*

- *Real talk about neglect, survival, and humor as armor*

- *Sarcasm thicker than LA smog in '92*

If you're looking for a sanitized, inspirational story about how adversity builds character, close the book and go read Chicken Soup for Someone Else's Soul.

This is for the ones who ate cereal out of Tupperware while watching Rescue 911.

The ones who got bullied at school and still had to rewind the damn VHS tape before returning it.

The ones who turned out okay-ish despite absolutely no adult supervision, emotional literacy, or sunscreen.

This is Gen X.

And this is how we lived, laughed, and barely processed any of it.

Welcome to the ride.

Hope you brought PB&J and some hose water. Let's go.

~ 1 ~

LATCHKEY NATION

Home Alone, Hungry, and Hella Resourceful

Growing up in the '80s was a wild, lawless time. Like, actual chaos disguised as childhood. I mean, they used to run real-deal commercials on TV that asked, "It's 10 PM—do you know where your kids are?" That wasn't a joke. That was a PSA. Because apparently, enough parents in America didn't know where the hell their kids were that someone in a suit had to greenlight a reminder.

This was the era before cell phones. And I don't mean iPhones, we're talkin' prehistoric communication bricks the size of a lunchbox. Or worse, car phones. Yes, kids, there was a time when the *car* had the phone and you didn't get to take it inside. You just stared at it longingly through the window like it was a toy you couldn't touch. We'll talk about the car phone saga later. Trust me.

Back then, parenting was less of a full-time job and more of a long-distance suggestion. Our parents would straight-up launch us into the day like underprepared astronauts. Especially in the summer. They'd throw together a peanut butter sandwich, maybe toss in a Capri Sun, hand you a dollar if they were feeling generous, and say, "Be home before the streetlights come on."

We weren't raised. We were *released.*

And we lived by a code. Not some noble Jedi code. No, I'm talking about a half-imagined, zero-supervision, mostly-improvised street constitution written by sleep-deprived kids fueled by Tang and Pop Rocks.

These were the **unofficial, unspoken House Rules of the Latchkey Kid.** And if you broke one? You were either grounded, hospitalized, or suddenly the main character in a family meeting no one wanted.

Rule #1: Lock the door behind you.

Except we didn't. Not really. You were *supposed* to, but half the time you left it cracked for your friends to sneak in through. Sometimes we'd even prop it open with a shoe, like we were running a 7-Eleven with no inventory.

Rule #2: Don't answer the phone unless you know who it is.

And by "know," I mean there was a whole-ass *system.* Two rings, pause, then one short ring? That was my dad. One ring followed by two short ones? That was Patsy calling from Texas. No pattern? *Stranger danger.* Let that shit go to voicemail. Well, the answering machine. Same thing, just louder.

Rule #3: Do NOT use the stove.

This rule was basically made just for me. I had a habit of thinking anything could be cooked on high in under 5 minutes. Bacon? High. Spaghetti? High. Chicken nuggets? High and dry, baby. That knob was always twisted to the max like I was summoning the god of grease fires. And when things inevitably started to smoke, I did what any logical kid would do: turned off the stove, opened the window, and started *fanning the air with a paper plate.*

Rule #4: Microwave mastery was life or death.

You learned quickly what you could and couldn't microwave. Tin foil? Congratulations, you just invented indoor lightning. Eggs in the shell? Now you're cleaning scrambled bomb fragments out of the roof. Hot dogs split open like they were in an action movie. Leftover pizza turned into a soggy roof shingle. But we ate it. Because that's what survival looked like.

Rule #5: If you break it, fix it—or hide the evidence.

Wobbly table leg? Stick a book under it and pretend it's always been that way. Crack in the window? Blame a rogue baseball. TV remote doesn't work anymore? Hide it in the couch and act surprised when Dad finds it three weeks later covered in Cheeto dust.

Rule #6: Clean up... but only what's visible.

We cleaned like raccoons with a deadline. Push it all under the bed. Cram it in the closet. Spray air freshener like it was holy water. If the house *looked* clean, it was clean. That was the law. Just don't let anyone open a drawer or check behind the couch.

Rule #7: Don't let anyone in.

Every parent said this. Every latchkey kid ignored it at least once. It was always someone—your neighbor, a school friend, a weird kid who claimed he had a Sega but couldn't prove it. Next thing you know, there's six people in your living room watching "Robocop" with the volume low and the VCR set to eject at the first sound of car tires in the driveway.

Rule #8: The couch is your throne. Protect it.

You claimed that spot the second you walked in. You had a setup—pillow fort, blanket cape, snacks within reach. If a sibling tried to move you, it was *war*. Remote control possession was nine-tenths of the law, and if you lost it, you were dead until the next commercial break.

Rule #9: Never admit to anything. Ever.

It doesn't matter if your fingerprints are on the wall or your name is spelled out in ketchup on the floor. DENY. Everything. Your job as a latchkey kid was not to confess—it was to redirect, deflect, and disappear. If it wasn't caught on Polaroid, it didn't happen.

Rule #10: If all else fails, fake sleep.

Parent storms in? Face down, TV off, eyes shut. Doesn't matter if it's 4 in the afternoon and "DuckTales" is still echoing through the room. If they think you're asleep, you bought yourself time. Time to plan. Time to shift blame. Time to *vanish*.

These were our commandments. Not written in stone, but probably in Sharpie on a Trapper Keeper. We didn't need helicopter parents. We had instincts. We had hustle. And we had a working knowledge of how to microwave a Pop-Tart without catching the kitchen on fire.

Mostly.

When my parents divorced, my mom dipped out to Texas like she'd just robbed a government building. Took my sisters with her. Left me behind. That hurt. That was probably the last time my bio mom and I were truly close.

My dad, though? He scooped me up without hesitation. Dude was a truck driver at the time and decided to relocate to California. Best. Decision. Ever.

We didn't move somewhere glamorous like L.A. or San Fran-
cisco. Nah, we landed in Sunnyvale. Back then, ain't nobody outside the Bay knew what or where Sunnyvale was. But to me? It was
California. That was enough.

My dad switched gigs and became a garbage man. And if you're
thinking that would've embarrassed me, you're wrong. Dead
wrong. Because my dad had routes that hit toy stores and toy fac-
tories. Which meant he regularly came home with bags of loot. I'm
talkin' G1 Transformers, action figures, random pieces of toy gold.
All free. All mine.

But since his workday started before sunrise, that meant mornings were all me. I was solo. That latchkey life hit real quick. He
made sure I knew how to walk to school, Cumberland Elementary
was just a block away, so even my scatterbrained self could handle
it. Barely.

I'd wake up, watch cartoons, grab my lunch, and roll out with
the Rios brothers, my first California friends. I don't even remember which one was in my class. What I do remember is one of them
collected matches. Like, actual matchbooks. I thought that was the
coolest thing ever. So naturally, I started collecting them too. Like
a tiny pyro-in-training.

My dad didn't notice. Not at first.

Then one day, I was in my room, striking matches just to watch
them burn. Yeah. I was really that dumb. I heard my dad come
home early and panicked. So what did I do? I threw the lit match
into my cardboard toy box.

Yup. The one filled with those dope-ass G1 Transformers. Cheap '80s plastic. Basically napalm with articulation. It went up fast. The whole room lit up like the Challenger.

And before anyone gets sensitive...yes, I know the Challenger explosion was tragic. We *all* watched it in school. They dragged a TV in and made us watch astronauts die before our first recess. So if I make jokes, just know that's how I cope.

Anyway, I'm standing there, nine years old, watching my room go full Michael Bay. Flames, smoke, melting Autobots. I earned an arson record that day—not legally, but my dad made sure I never lived it down. Forever the firebug. Latchkey edition.

Now, you'd think being left alone and accidentally committing toy box arson would be the worst part of my childhood. Nah. Let me introduce you to the hellscape of being the *middle* child *and* the only boy.

Patsy came first in '76. I was born in '77. Lindsay joined the crew in '79. Which means from the jump, I was flanked. Outnumbered. And often outvoted. My sisters were my best friends and my first enemies. They jumped me more than once growing up. They also never let me forget I was the middle kid, the one nobody asked for. Like a bonus track nobody asked for but still showed up on the album anyway, just hangin' out at the end, confusing everybody.

Let's talk birthdays.

I was born August 25, 1977. Lindsay? August 20, 1979. Five days apart. That meant I had two, count 'em, TWO years of solo birthday shine before she rolled in and hijacked my whole situation.

And for most of my childhood, I didn't even realize we had separate birthdays. Because the party was always hers. Her name on the invites. Her cake. Her friends. Every damn year.

One year, I looked at a mountain of presents and told my dad, "Wow! So many people came to celebrate Lindsay and me!"

My man didn't say a word.

Wanna know why? Not one single gift was for me. They'd forgotten to include me on the invites.

My mom panicked, ran into the kitchen, and came back out with a box wrapped in paper. I opened it, thinking it might be a last-minute save.

It was a box of cereal.

Not a fun cereal. Not Lucky Charms or Cocoa Pebbles. No.

Cheerios.

Plain-ass, paper-flavored, yellow-box Cheerios. The kind that tastes like regret and broken promises.

To this day, I won't let that box in my house. You bring Cheerios into my kitchen, I will escort them out like a bouncer at a club. That's not breakfast, it's edible trauma.

Now if you think that was a one-time mistake, oh no. Let's talk Christmas 1984.

We were the first American-born kids in our family. Our dad, grandma, aunts, uncles, all from Mexico. We were the grand experiment. And most of the time, we were spoiled. But not that year.

My grandma...who I absolutely adore...wanted to get each of us something special.

Patsy wanted a Cabbage Patch Kid.

Lindsay asked for Rainbow Brite or My Little Pony.

Me? I wanted Superman. The Kenner Super Powers figure *with* his flying ship.

Yeah, I know. Superman can fly. He doesn't need a ship. But don't bring logic into this. I was all in.

Christmas Eve at my grandma's house on Allen. Three boxes under the tree. My dad, in full "ladies first" mode, gave the green light.

Lindsay opens hers...BOOM. Rainbow Brite *and* the pony. She's glowing.

Patsy goes next and gets a bald-ass Cabbage Patch Preemie, straight from the Kmart hookup (my aunt worked there). My aunt didn't even have to fight for it. Must've been a slow shopping day.

Then me.

Right as I reach for my box, my uncle slips me a ten-dollar bill and says, "Sorry, nephew."

Didn't register. I thought it was just a bonus.

I unwrap the box... and it's not the bright Kenner packaging I dreamed about. It's brown. Just... brown.

I open it.

One. Single. Walkie. Talkie.

No second unit. No batteries. Just a lone device designed to speak to absolutely no one. That was my gift.

Turns out my grandma forgot to buy mine, and by the time she remembered, Superman was sold out. The walkie-talkie was her last-minute save.

They say I handled it well. Didn't cry. Didn't flip out.

Yeah, because I was in shock. I had no emotional system in place for *that* level of betrayal.

That, my friends, was my supervillain origin story.

It took thirty-seven years to right that wrong. But when it finally happened? You better believe it was glorious.

This book? Part memoir. Part cautionary tale. Part Gen X survival manual. You'll get serious moments, sure. But mostly, this is about growing up feral, figuring it out, and laughing through the scars. We didn't just survive—we adapted. We evolved. We watched "Unsolved Mysteries" while eating raw Top Ramen and lived to tell the story.

Pop culture wasn't just a part of growing up Gen X — it *was* our third parent. The one that never checked in on us, let us stay up too late, and raised us with reruns, one-liners, and iconic theme songs. It didn't hug us, but it *did* teach us what love looked like through John Hughes movies and Lionel Richie videos.

We didn't have social media or a 24-hour feed of everyone's thoughts. We had music videos that *meant* something, and shows that felt like secret clubs. You weren't cool because you had followers. You were cool because you memorized the Fresh Prince theme song, could quote "Ferris Bueller's Day Off" line for line, and knew which Ninja Turtle matched your personality.

Pop culture told us how to talk, dress, flirt, rebel, and survive. It was how we bonded. If someone didn't understand your "Saved by the Bell" reference or couldn't name the core members of New Edition, they simply weren't your people. If someone couldn't name every character on *He-Man*, *Jem*, or *Voltron*, we questioned their whole upbringing.

We watched music evolve on MTV, when it actually played music. We lived through the pain of trying to record a mixtape from the radio, only to have the DJ yell the station name over your favorite intro. We survived the trauma of having *one TV* in the house and *no remote*. You *were* the remote.

We learned life lessons from sitcoms that did a hard pivot into "Very Special Episode" mode without warning. One minute it's all laughs and catchphrases, the next we're dealing with alcoholism, stranger danger, or the horror of having a classmate bring a gun to school. These episodes traumatized us *and* taught us something—usually while we were still eating pizza rolls.

And don't even get me started on the After School Specials. The titles read like emotional landmines: *I Think I'm Having a Baby, Mom, I Can't Breathe, The Day My Kid Went Punk*. If those titles don't sound familiar, you probably still have hope in your soul. But if you *do* remember them? Welcome. You are among the damaged and de-lightful.

And hey, we're just scratching the surface here. We haven't even gotten into Saturday morning cartoon dominance, the power of the mall food court, the rise of home video stores, the impor-tance of theme song choreography, or why everyone in Gen X thinks the word "Turbo" makes anything cooler. That's all coming in later chapters.

So yeah. This book is going to reference a *lot* of pop culture. Not because it's trendy, but because for Gen X...it was *everything*. Our comfort food. Our emotional compass. Our babysitter, teacher, therapist, and hype man.

We didn't just grow up with pop culture. We inhaled it, memo-rized it, and *became* it.

Also, you're gonna hear me talk about a lot of people doing re-ally stupid fucking things in this book. Patsy and Lindsay are my real sisters, and I'm using their real names—because the statute of limitations has *got* to have worn off by now. Everyone else? Yeah, I'm changing names. Not because I'm scared. I just don't need legal trouble messing with my snack time.

Now let's see how deep the rabbit hole really goes.

~ 2 ~

I WANT MY MTV

August 1, 1981. I was only three years old, probably still trying to figure out how to color inside the lines, but something massive had just entered the universe. MTV. And no, that didn't stand for "Mostly Trashy Videos" or "Mediocre Teen Vomit" like it feels today. It stood for Music Television. A revolutionary idea back then. But it would take a couple more years before that loud, wild, culture-defining beast would become part of my daily life, and ultimately help raise me.

My first glimpse of MTV wasn't even on a screen. It was a logo on a t-shirt. My Uncle Ruben had one in 1983 with that chunky, colorful MTV emblem printed across the chest. It looked loud. It looked cool. I didn't know what it was, but I wanted in. At that point in my life, my playlist consisted of certified toddler bangers like "The Wheels on the Bus" and "If You're Happy and You Know It." But then I heard something that flipped a switch in my little kid brain: "Jump" by Van Halen. I didn't know what genre it was. All I knew was that it slapped. I didn't realize it at the time, but that was the moment I fell in love with music—and MTV was about to become my gateway drug.

Then it happened. December 2, 1983. My uncles gathered around the TV like it was the Super Bowl. Michael Jackson was about to debut something called "Thriller." I wedged myself between them, trying to figure out what all the hype was about. And then... boom. Zombies. Fog. Vincent Price's creepy voice. And that jacket. It wasn't just a music video—it was a short film. A whole-ass cinematic event. That was the first moment MTV burned itself into my brain. After that, I was all in.

MTV became my daily ritual. My portal into a world that felt so much cooler than anything I had around me. Prince. Run-DMC. Aerosmith. Duran Duran. Madonna. Every video was like a message from another dimension, one where people dressed wild, said whatever they wanted, and didn't apologize for taking up space.

MTV didn't just show you music, it showed you *how to feel it.* How to move. How to dress. How to rebel.

And let's just address the glitter-covered elephant in the room. Yes, Michael Jackson was the King of Pop, and yes, *Thriller* was the cultural atom bomb that shook the world. But make no mistake, this household flew the purple flag. We were Team Prince. MJ wanted to be a god. Prince wanted to be a revolution and he *was.*

Michael had the moonwalk. Prince had mystique. MJ had Neverland. Prince had Paisley Park, his purple funk fortress where the walls sweat sex and sound. While Michael gave us perfect pop choreography, Prince gave us guitar solos that bled emotion, lyrics so filthy the church side-eyed him, and looks that broke gender and fashion all in one go. MJ wanted to entertain you. Prince wanted to awaken you.

When Michael passed in 2009, the world mourned with sequins and spin moves. When Prince passed in 2016, the sky went purple. He didn't just die—he *evaporated*, leaving behind glitter, silence, and a catalog so untouchable it made other legends look like opening acts. And if you ever doubted how magical he was, just remember: the Dave Chappelle skit about him dunking on Charlie Murphy in a blouse? That wasn't parody. That was historical documentation. He served pancakes after humiliating people in a pickup game. That's divine energy.

Then came *Yo! MTV Raps.* And everything exploded again. This show didn't just showcase a genre—it gave us a cultural education. Digital Underground, Ice Cube, LL Cool J, Queen Latifah, A Tribe Called Quest. And then 2Pac showed up like a prophecy in motion. Hip-hop had a home now. And I had a soundtrack for every part of my emotional chaos. Mad? There was a video. In love? A video. Depressed, hype, bored, confused? MTV had something for every vibe and a look to match.

My first real crush? Martha Quinn. Followed closely by Nina Blackwood. I didn't know what sexual tension was yet, but they made me feel things. JJ Jackson and Mark Goodman were cooler than any adult I knew. These VJs were our big siblings—funny, edgy, and always in the know. We didn't just want to be musicians. We wanted to be them.

The 90s arrived, and MTV went into full beast mode. This was their golden era when every weird, wonderful corner of youth culture had its own show. It was a buffet of subcultures, and if you were lucky, you got a little taste of everything.

But the crown jewel? The MTV Beach House.

Let me explain something for those too young to know: the MTV Beach House was the dream. It wasn't just a location, it was a whole damn vibe. Every summer, MTV would rent out some sun-drenched, oceanside mansion, stick a bunch of VJs in board shorts and bikini tops, and let the cameras roll. There were impromptu concerts, celebrity guests, dance contests, water balloon fights, and interviews that felt like poolside hangouts. It was chaos, but it was fun chaos, you know the kind that made you want to climb inside your TV screen and cannonball into the pool.

We'd sit on our stained couches, slurping ice pops in front of box fans, watching these beautiful, wild older kids live out our fantasy life. The Beach House wasn't just cool, it was aspirational. It made every Gen X kid dream of someday growing up, getting a tan, and being ridiculous on cable for a living.

And then there was Spring Break.

MTV Spring Break was the Super Bowl of teenage rebellion. Broadcast live from places like Daytona Beach, Cancun, or South Padre Island, this was where the chaos turned up to 11. Live performances from your favorite bands and rappers, barely clothed dance contests, foam parties, questionable decision-making—it had it all. It was sexy, sweaty, loud, and impossible to look away from.

For those of us stuck at home, Spring Break was a weeklong peek into a parallel universe where everyone was hot, horny, and somehow not failing algebra. We'd gather with our friends, shout at the TV, and swear that one day, *that* would be us—doing the worm on stage next to a guy in JNCOs while Sisqó performed in the background. MTV made us believe that adulthood was one big beach party waiting to happen.

Spoiler alert: it wasn't. But it was one hell of a dream.

But MTV wasn't just escapism, it was identity-shaping. It was where Gen X kids learned to question authority, embrace weirdness, and trust that their emotions, however messy were valid.

It was also where we first saw culture shift in real time. MTV didn't just reflect youth culture, it helped *shape* it. Through shows like *Rock the Vote*, it politicized a generation without sounding like a lecture. It made voting cool...at least for a hot minute. Through *The Real World*, especially with Pedro Zamora, it introduced us to queer identity and the devastating impact of HIV/AIDS with more compassion than most school systems could ever offer. It gave us artists like Salt-N-Pepa who taught us that women could be sexy *and* in control, and artists like Public Enemy and Rage Against the Machine who shouted truth to power loud enough to rattle suburban living rooms. MTV helped us unlearn and relearn the world—one video at a time. We didn't have therapy. We had *Unplugged*. We didn't have TED Talks. We had *Beavis and Butt-Head*. MTV was our classroom, and it taught in chaos, color, and chorus hooks.

It gave us *The Grind* when we needed to shake it off, *Headbangers Ball* when we needed to rage, and *Daria* when we were emotionally unavailable but still wanted to be understood.

By the time I was 12, I had a full-on ritual. MTV Jams with Bill Bellamy came on at 7:30 AM, and you best believe I was front and center. That show set the mood. Smooth R&B joints, hip-hop bangers, videos that made you want to fall in love, or at least pretend to. I'd watch until it was time to head to school, but if I was home sick or it was summer vacation? It was an *all-day* affair. MTV stayed on like background radiation.

Sometimes the squad would pull up, and we'd post up in the living room, watching videos and roasting each other, arguing about who had better taste. And yeah...I was usually trying to mack on one or more of my sisters' friends. I thought I was living my *Mambo No. 5* era when in reality, I was deep in the trenches of DMX's *What These Bitches Want*. I had a big thing for one of their friends, let's just call her Kay. Obviously not her real name, but if she's reading this, she knows I'm talking about her. We dated on and off for a few years before we both moved on to better things. These days, we'll exchange a message here or there on social media, but that chapter's long since closed.

MTV was like church to a lot of us. Whether it was *MTV Jams*, *Headbangers Ball*, *Yo! MTV Raps*, *Remote Control* (a truly underrated game show we *absolutely* need to bring back), or the raw animated chaos of *Beavis and Butt-Head* and *Aeon Flux*, MTV had something for everyone. It wasn't just a channel—it was a community center, a confessional booth, and a chaotic cultural compass all in one. It gave us freedom in the form of eyeliner, flannel shirts, and way too much Aqua Net.

And then, like every great love story... it changed.

Enter: *The Real World.*

Let me be real—it was genius. The original intro is tattooed in our collective memory: "This is the true story... of seven strangers... picked to live in a house..." And just like that, the era of reality TV was born. MTV dipped a toe in—and then swan-dived straight into the shallow end. The music slowly faded into the background. Then it disappeared altogether.

By the late 90s, *TRL* was still holding the torch, but it was flickering. Music became a side dish to the main course of messy drama and beautiful people fighting in hot tubs. I was in college by this point, too busy juggling bills and heartbreak to keep tuning in every day. MTV faded from vital to optional.

Then came the 2000s, and the death rattle. Music videos were exiled to 3AM time slots. Daytime TV was now *Laguna Beach*, *The Hills*, and *My Super Sweet 16* aka rich-kid melodrama on loop. I tuned back in, hoping for a glimpse of the channel that raised me. What I found was wall-to-wall *Ridiculousness*. No soul. Just reruns.

MTV turned 30 and didn't even throw itself a damn party. No countdown of iconic moments. No tribute to the moon landing opening. And when it turned 40? Same deal. Just more looped-out trash and missed opportunities. Like someone unplugged the magic and left it buffering for a decade.

Now it's 2025. MTV is 44. And while I'm out here trying to age like a smooth bourbon, MTV aged like a warm jug of gas station milk. It doesn't recognize itself anymore. And maybe that's the saddest part, we all grew up, but MTV forgot how.

Still... I remember.

I remember when it mattered. I remember when the music videos made me believe. When the VJs felt like friends. When rebellion came wrapped in lace, leather, and a badass guitar solo.

I remember when MTV was *everything.*

~ 3 ~

STYLE WARS

*W**here the only real fashion rule was: Don't look broke... even if you were.*

Growing up Gen X meant you were drafted into a lifelong war the moment you figured out how to lace up your own shoes. But this wasn't a war with guns and grenades—this was a war of **style**. And it was brutal. Ruthless. Petty. Political. And every damn bit of it mattered.

You either had the shoes... or you didn't.

You either wore name brand... or you got clowned.

You either understood the assignment... or you ended up in the lost and found emotionally.

Style wasn't just about fashion. It was about **survival**. Your jeans, your jacket, your backpack, even the brand of your deodorant if anyone caught a whiff—all of it sent signals about who you were, where you stood, and whether or not you were gonna get roasted into oblivion by lunch.

This chapter is about the fights fought in locker rooms, lunch tables, and bus stops across America. About knockoff trauma, starter jacket heists, and why a certain pair of Jordans could make you a god... or a ghost.

We'll talk:

- The reign of **Z. Cavaricci** and why those pants were somehow both elite and ridiculous.

- The **starter jacket era**—and how kids were legit catching beatdowns just for wearing the wrong team in the wrong zip code.

- The rise of **Cross Colours, FUBU, Karl Kani, and Tommy**... and what they said about race, pride, and flex.

- How Gen X fashion was influenced by hip-hop, grunge, skate culture, and whatever was being served up on MTV that week.

- That unspoken but fully understood rule: **You could be weird, poor, or loud—but you couldn't be all three.**

We'll also unpack:

- My own fashion fails (including that time I wore British Knights thinking I was killing it... spoiler: I was not)

- My sisters' impact on my style (and their relentless slander)

- And the politics of the hallway catwalk: how every walk to class felt like you were being judged by the Supreme Court of Cool.

Fashion in the Gen X era wasn't curated for a feed, it was fought for in the trenches. And your style didn't come with a stylist. It came from hand-me-downs, thrift store miracles, or the one aunt who let you pick *one* name brand item from Mervyn's for back to school. This was survival by swagger.

So go ahead, lace up your L.A. Gear, slap on that Hypercolor tee, and try not to get roasted for rocking Pro Wings.

It's time to step into the arena.

The Hair Bears: Aqua Net and Attitude

OK, Patsy, as you are reading this understand the following. I love you, sis. I really truly do. BUT I am about to straight up roast some of your more hilarious fashion choices.

See, my sister was a queen of many things in the late 80s. She was the undisputed queen of Aqua Net hairspray. If you are unfamiliar with the legend of Aqua Net, let me break it down for you: a 6 ft tall can of hairspray, a liquid that could easily freeze a dinosaur in time, and it only cost 99 cents. I mean this shit was so serious that if you lit a match in the vicinity of one of the Hair Bears, chances are it would go up like my room in '87, fiery inferno.

These girls had bangs that defied physics. We're talking about teased, torqued, shellacked masterpieces of geometry. Bangs that looked less like hair and more like architectural structures. These weren't just styles. These were front-facing awnings of intimidation. Step under those bangs, and you might find shade, secrets, and a cloud of aerosol with enough chemical power to reboot the ozone layer.

They would carry a brush in one back pocket and the holy grail—Aqua Net—in the other. Class change? Boom. Quick flip, pull out the can, and *pssshhhht* - like clockwork. It didn't even matter if they were indoors. Fire code? Never heard of her. You could be in the middle of the cafeteria and suddenly catch a puff of hairspray strong enough to pickle your retinas.

You had the Low Bears - girls who kept it simple, bangs curled under but still lacquered to hell. The Mid Bears—those were the ones who teased just enough to hit cheekbone level. And then...the High Bears. The elite. The legends. The ones whose bangs were so tall they could throw off your line of sight in math class. These girls would duck walking into a room just so their bang tower didn't hit the top of the doorframe.

And don't even try to talk slick to a Hair Bear. You think you're ready for verbal combat, but you're not. These girls were fast with the clapbacks and faster with the can. One minute you're cracking jokes, next minute your eyebrows are sticky and you're rethinking your whole life.

Patsy, you were a High Bear. And I say that with pride. You walked so today's influencers could run. Except you didn't need a ring light or a filter—you had Aqua Net and attitude. Respect the legacy.

The Starter Jacket Era: Flex and Fear in Equal Measure

There was a time in the early 90s when owning a Starter jacket wasn't just a fashion choice—it was a full-blown social currency.

These satin-coated, logo-heavy, team-branded masterpieces were the crown jewels of middle and high school wardrobes across America. And don't get it twisted—this wasn't just about repping your favorite team. No, sir. This was about status. Swagger. Survival.

You could be wearing a Raiders Starter jacket in California and instantly become *that dude*. Or a Bulls one and get mad respect just by channeling MJ's greatness. But there was always a catch. That same jacket that made you feel invincible walking through the halls could make you a walking target the minute you stepped off campus.

There were kids getting *jumped* for their Starter jackets. People getting pressed by older kids or straight-up robbed. I'm not exaggerating. It got so bad in some places that schools had to ban them outright. Imagine being banned for having too much sauce. That was the power of the Starter.

You couldn't just wear *any* team, either. Rock a Cowboys or Raiders jacket in the wrong neighborhood and suddenly you weren't making a fashion statement—you were making enemies. It was gang-adjacent whether you liked it or not. You had to know where you were, what street you were on, and who might be watching. All because of a damn coat.

And shoutout to the kids who wore the Hornets jacket strictly for the teal and purple drip. You had no allegiance to Charlotte, you just liked the colors—and honestly, I respect it.

The Air Jordan Era: Walk Like a God, Pay Like a Mortal

Let's talk about the holy grail. The undisputed championship belt of Gen X fashion. Air. Freakin'. Jordans.

If Starter jackets were the crown, then Jordans were the throne. These weren't just shoes. These were anointings. When you wore Jordans, you weren't just walking to class—you were gliding. Floating. The halls parted. The crowd noticed. You didn't even have to be good at basketball. Your vertical didn't matter. Just wearing them made you *feel* like you could dunk from half court and win the game at the buzzer.

The first pair I saw in real life felt like I was witnessing something divine. The leather, the detail, the weight of them, everything screamed, "You can't afford me, but you will worship me." And we did.

You knew the kids who had the latest pair because they made sure you knew. There was no walking quietly in Jordans. They stomped down the hallway like the shoes were powered by confidence and child support.

But oh, the drama if you dared to scuff them. The *pain*. The ritual cleaning with a toothbrush. The agony if someone stepped on them. Fights have started. Friendships ended. I once saw a kid stop mid-kickball game just to take off his brand-new Jordans and play the rest in socks. That's how serious it was.

And if you couldn't afford real ones? Welcome to the land of Payless knockoffs and quiet shame. We tried to pass them off, but the truth always came out. Somebody always spotted the difference. The colors were just slightly off. The jumpman looked like he had scoliosis. Game over.

If you had a Starter jacket *and* Jordans? That was peak elite. That was god-tier. That was walking into school like you had your own theme music. And it better be Public Enemy or LL Cool J, because otherwise you were wasting it.

Z. Cavaricci, IOU, and the Peak of Pants Arrogance

Let's talk about pants with more attitude than most people. Enter: **Z. Cavaricci.** These weren't pants, they were declarations. High-waisted, pleated, and buckled like you were headed to either a nightclub or a board meeting run by Vanilla Ice. You didn't wear Z. Cavariccis to blend in, you wore them to *be seen*. And we saw you.

The belt came built in, the legs ballooned like you were smuggling air, and the taper at the ankle? Sharp enough to slice egos. You needed confidence, cologne, and probably a full can of mousse just to survive a school day in those bad boys. If you didn't have at least one pair, you were a nobody in the eyes of the cafeteria elite.

And then there was **IOU**. Now that was an entire era of pastel confusion and oversized dreams. IOU sweatshirts were the uniform of every kid who wanted to feel like they owned a yacht but had never seen the ocean. The fabric? Thick enough to survive a nuclear winter. The letters? Blocky enough to be seen from space. We had no clue what IOU stood for, but we wore it like it was sponsored by NASA.

Guess Jeans and the Golden Triangle of Popularity

Guess jeans weren't clothes. They were status symbols. That little triangle on the butt pocket meant you had either 1) rich parents, 2) a cousin who stole for you, or 3) an angel who floated you one glorious back-to-school shopping spree. There was no in-between.

Guess didn't care about your comfort. That denim was stiff enough to sand drywall. But it didn't matter. If you had the triangle, you walked taller. Sat straighter. Got invited to more birthday parties. Especially if you paired it with... you already know... one strap down.

Overalls with One Strap Down: The Official Uniform of "I'm Cool but Casual"

This trend? Legendary. You rocked your overalls with one strap fastened and the other flapping like a denim cape of rebellion. Bonus points if you wore a neon shirt underneath or a Cross Colours tee. This was the look that said, "Yeah, I have homework... but I also might be in Kriss Kross." We all did it. It was effortless cool, which of course meant it actually took forever to get that one strap to sit just right without snapping you like a mousetrap.

Kriss Kross and the Backwards Wardrobe Delusion

Speaking of Kriss Kross...what the actual fuck were we thinking?

I mean, one day we dead ass decided that *today* was the day we would wear all our clothes backwards. Shirts, pants, overalls, jackets, if it had a front, we turned it around like our wardrobes owed us money. And this seemed like a solid plan at first. Like we were joining a revolution. We were *cool*. We were *different*.

But let's be real. By second period, every one of us was in the locker room, sweating bullets and wrestling with zippers that were no longer accessible. The novelty wore off *fast*, especially when you realized that going to the bathroom in backwards jeans was a full Olympic event. God help you if you had to go after the cafeteria pizza declared jihad on your GI tract.

That bathroom panic? That's when the rebellion ended. That's when we looked in the mirror and realized...this isn't cool. This is a hostage situation sewn in denim. It was the shortest-lived trend with the longest-lasting embarrassment. And yet... for a brief, shining moment, we all believed.

The Roll and Tuck: Because Hemming Was for Suckers

Ah yes, the roll-and-tuck cuff. Why go to a tailor when you had thumbs and time? You'd fold your jeans at the ankle, roll them up twice, and boom - instant style. This technique made your legs look weirdly shaped but also guaranteed you wouldn't get your Jordans dirty. Priorities.

It was a flex if done right, and a tragedy if done wrong. One sloppy cuff and you were getting roasted all day. Bonus humiliation if someone walked by and unrolled one on purpose. That was a friendship-ending move. But the roll-and-tuck lived on because it was DIY fashion. It was working-class swag. It was us saying, "We see your designer tailoring and raise you $12 jeans and raw determination."

Hypercolor: The Mood Ring of T-Shirts

Let's take a moment to talk about one of the weirdest, wildest, and most unnecessary fashion experiments of the Gen X era...**Hypercolor shirts**.

In theory, these shirts were the future. You put them on and *boom,* they changed color with heat. Your body temp, someone's handprint, a random gust of air or whatever triggered a temp shift, your shirt would show it. Science! Magic! Fashion!

Except... it was never the color you *wanted.* You started off in a nice shade of teal, and by third period you looked like someone had sneezed hot lava across your chest. Armpits? Instant heat maps. Back sweat? Fully displayed. Hypercolor didn't hide anything. It exposed *everything.*

And don't let someone smack you on the back, you were walking around with a human handprint for the rest of the day. There was no escape. These shirts turned middle school hallways into living thermometers.

Worse yet, they faded *fast.* One trip through mom's washer and dryer and that Hypercolor magic was gone forever. Now you just had a weird, discolored shirt that looked like it had trauma.

But for a minute? We were obsessed. It was science and style in one. It said, "I'm cool, I'm futuristic, and I am definitely going to regret this by lunch."

Another bold experiment by the greatest generation of fashion test dummies ever assembled.

BUM Equipment: Bold, Unapologetic, and Everywhere

Let's give a shoutout to **BUM Equipment,** the brand that made it completely normal to walk around with the word "BUM" plastered across your chest in the boldest damn font imaginable. You had to have a certain level of confidence—or zero self-aware-ness—to rock that logo like a badge of honor.

These sweatshirts were thick as hell, oversized by design, and somehow made you feel like both a badass and a walking billboard for questionable decisions. Didn't matter though. If you had a BUM sweatshirt, you *were* somebody. Or at least you *felt* like somebody for that fleeting week before the next big brand dropped.

You didn't just wear BUM Equipment, you leaned into it. You posed in school photos with it. You showed up to the roller rink with it. You got called "BUM" by teachers and classmates alike and still wore it proudly.

Let the Roast Commence: Gen X Fashion Crimes and Misde-meanors

I would love to sit here and say I was not roasted but that would be a bloody lie. I was indeed roasted mercilessly. I had some Pro Wings for a long time until my dad got tired of me fucking those trash ass sneakers up on purpose (which I did in protest until he got me some Jordans or Reebok Pumps). I was also blessed to be handed down my sister's IOU sweatshirt. So the PTSD from not only being the middle child spread to having to wear shit shoes and hand-me-downs until my dad realized that he would never see the family line continue as long as I looked like a garbage pail kid.

My glow-up, however, is the stuff of legend. But that story is for another time.

Okay, now that we've paid homage to the trends that ruled the school, let's keep it real and start the roast. Because Gen X fashion wasn't just iconic, it was *chaotic*.

We already talked about Kriss Kross, but seriously, what were we even doing? Waking up and deciding that backwards clothing was the move? Like, that was the hill we wanted to die on? It looked cool for all of five minutes, until we realized we couldn't pee without dislocating a hip or turning into Houdini.

Then there were the **Pro Wings warriors**. Look...I respect you now. I do. You were doing your best, and survival is survival. But back then? If you showed up in Pro Wings, you got roasted like the Thanksgiving turkey. Mercilessly. Loudly. Publicly. We were monsters and those poor souls took the heat like champs. You could've had a 4.0 GPA and cured chickenpox, but if your shoes said "Payless" instead of "Nike," your social life flatlined by recess.

Let's not forget **corduroy**. The enemy of stealth. You weren't sneaking up on *anyone* in those pants. A deaf person could hear you coming from three hallways away. It was like rubbing two loofahs together at full speed. And if you dared wear tight corduroy? Now you were both loud *and* awkward. Congratulations.

But the *ultimate* kiss of death? Rocking **bootleg brands**. You know exactly what I'm talking about—those fake Tommy shirts that said "Tommy Hilfinger" or a Calvin Klein that mysteriously spelled it "Kelvin Clain." If you got caught wearing one of those, the hallway tribunal opened court immediately. You'd hear someone shout "Bro, that ain't real!" and from there it was a full roast session. No mercy. Zero chill. And if you tried to defend it? That just made it worse. Now you were getting clowned *and* pitied.

Gen X didn't have cyberbullying. We had hallway humiliation, and it was instant, live, and unrelenting. You wore the wrong fit, you got lit up. The end.

But you know what? Those days built character. Fashion faux pas were rites of passage. We survived, we learned, and we came out of it with stories funnier than anything TikTok could manufacture.

Long live the roast. Long live Gen X.

~ 4 ~

WE ATE LIKE WE HAD A DEATH WISH

Pop Culture Anchors: Ecto Cooler, Crystal Pepsi, Dunkaroos, Ninja Turtle Pies, Mountain Dew, Sprite Ads with Hip-Hop Legends

We didn't eat to live. We ate to vibe. Gen X was raised on a diet that looked like it was made by sleep-deprived cartoon animators and FDA scientists who had just given up. Our food glowed in the dark, changed colors when it shouldn't, and often came with collectible pogs or a random plastic toy embedded inside like a choking hazard roulette.

There was no Whole Foods. No one knew what gluten was. We had Wonder Bread that could be compressed into a baseball and meat so processed it might've once been a couch cushion. But goddamn, it was glorious.

THE MORNING CHAOS: CEREAL, TOAST, AND TANG

If breakfast was the most important meal of the day, then the 80s and 90s cereal game was a straight-up sugar-coated psychological operation. These boxes weren't food — they were art. They were propaganda. Bright colors, cartoon mascots, free toys inside, mazes and trivia on the back. Every box screamed **"Pick me or you're a loser."**

We weren't just eating cereal — we were declaring our identity.

Let's be honest: most of the cereals Gen X ate were just *desserts in disguise*. These brands weren't trying to sneak nutrition in. They were trying to out-sugar each other like they were in a gladiator pit. It wasn't "how much fiber does it have?" It was "how many marshmallows can we legally cram in here before the FDA shuts us down?"

Here's the wild lineup:

- **Fruity Pebbles**: They looked like aquarium gravel and turned your milk radioactive, but the flavor slapped so hard it was worth the sogginess after 90 seconds.

- **Cocoa Pebbles**: Basically drinking chocolate milk with crunch. Addictive. A boulder of pure cocoa chaos.

- **Lucky Charms**: "Part of a balanced breakfast" if your idea of balance was straight sugar and marshmallow unicorn crack.

- **Trix**: Only for kids, allegedly. Balls of artificial fruit that tasted like betrayal once they "upgraded" to real fruit flavor. No thanks.

- **Cap'n Crunch**: This shit didn't just crunch — it *attacked*. It destroyed the roof of your mouth and you STILL went back for more.

- **Cinnamon Toast Crunch**: The thinking kid's sugar bomb. Real cinnamon. Real sugar. And commercials that suggested the cereal was *cannibalistic*. We didn't care.

- **Cookie Crisp**: Cookies. For breakfast. That's it. That's the whole pitch. And it *worked*.

- **Reese's Puffs**: You like candy? Here's a bowl of it. Peanut butter and chocolate flavor explosions at 7 AM. Your teacher didn't stand a chance.

- **French Toast Crunch**: Tiny fake pieces of bread that had no business tasting that good.

- **Waffle Crisp**: Even faker bread. Even more delicious. An ungodly syrup smell that filled the whole house like a sugar exorcism.

- **Sprinkle Spangles**: Because apparently *sprinkles* alone weren't enough. They needed their *own cereal*.

- **Oreo O's**: Why eat an Oreo when you can shovel an entire bowl of them in milk and call it breakfast?

- **Dunkin' Donuts Cereal**: Yes. This was real. Multiple flavors. It was dessert inception — a breakfast that was a cereal of a donut of a coffee shop.

- **Ice Cream Cones Cereal**: Because if donuts weren't enough, how about ice cream at 7 AM? Your pancreas never stood a chance.

Even the so-called "healthy" ones were a scam:

- **Honey Smacks** and **Golden Crisp**? They were basically caramelized frog bait.

- **Frosted Flakes**? Coated in so much sugar Tony the Tiger had you running laps before the bell even rang.

- **Apple Jacks**? Allegedly apple-flavored, but it was really just sweetened mystery dust.

And then came the **tie-in cereals** — the true collector's items.

- **Nintendo Cereal System**

- **Batman Cereal**

- **Addams Family Cereal**

- **Urkel-Os**

- **The Real Ghostbusters Cereal**

- **Teenage Mutant Ninja Turtles Cereal**

- **Barbie, G.I. Joe, Mr. T, The Smurfs, Pac-Man** — every brand slapped a mascot on a box and called it breakfast.

These cereals weren't just food. They were pop culture events. If your favorite show had a cereal, it was like Christmas morning every time you hit the cereal aisle.

Cereal in the Gen X era wasn't a meal. It was *battle prep.* You scarfed down two bowls of high-fructose chaos and hit school with pupils dilated, heart racing, and fingers still sticky from digging for the toy inside the box. And somehow... *we turned out fine.*

Sorta.

SUGAR BY THE SPOONFUL (AKA THE LEGAL COCAINE YEARS)

Before school nutrition guidelines, before gluten-free any-thing, before a single adult ever uttered the word "macros," Gen X kids were out here **freebasing sugar at the breakfast table.** And the adults? They either didn't notice or were too jacked on black coffee and cigarette fumes to care.

We weren't just *eating* sugar — we were inhaling it. By the god-damn spoonful.

Let's talk about the legends:

- **Tang**: This orange-flavored powder was allegedly in-vented for astronauts, but tasted like radioactive Sunny D fil-tered through a mouthful of nickels. It didn't "dissolve" — it *fought* the water. You had to stir that shit like a mad scientist just to get it to behave. But if it was good enough for NASA, it was good enough for us. Also, no one ever used the rec-ommended amount. We dumped in enough powder to turn it into **battery acid** and called it juice.

- **Carnation Instant Breakfast**: The name implied health. It was a lie. This was a straight-up chocolate milkshake in disguise. It promised vitamins, but what it *delivered* was a sugar rush so powerful it had you vibrating through math class.

- **Quik/Nesquik**: You know damn well we never measured. One heaping spoon turned into three, and suddenly you had sludge at the bottom of your milk like a chocolate quicksand trap. And don't even pretend you didn't scoop that sludge out with your finger like a caveman on a sugar bender.

- **Ovaltine**: This was marketed as the "wholesome" one. Lies. Ovaltine was just dusty-ass cocoa powder wearing a cardigan. It still hit — but let's not act like it was a multivitamin. It was a gateway powder, just like the rest.

- **Kool-Aid (Honorable Mention)**: Not a breakfast drink, but worth shouting out because we were adding **literal cups of sugar** to a packet of powder like we were building a bomb. The Kool-Aid Man didn't crash through walls because he was excited — he was jacked up on straight glucose and rage.

Bottom line: we weren't eating breakfast.

We were **free-running through a sugar rave** before school, and no one gave a damn.

By the time we hit the classroom, our blood sugar was spiking like a crypto chart. Teachers wondered why we couldn't sit still — bitch, we just drank rocket fuel and ate toaster candy.

BREAKFAST BLOODSPORT: POP-TARTS VS. TOASTER STRUDEL

Forget Ali vs. Frazier. Forget Pacquiao vs. Mayweather. This was the **real** heavyweight title fight of the Gen X breakfast table: **Pop-Tarts** vs. **Toaster Strudel**. A goddamn pastry war.

You either lived in a **Pop-Tart household** or a **Toaster Strudel household**. There was no Switzerland. There were no alliances. This was breakfast warfare with casualties and crumbs.

POP-TARTS: THE PEOPLE'S FUCKING CHAMP

Pop-Tarts were the scrappy, ride-or-die hero of the underdog generation.

They came in a box of twelve, cost like three bucks, and didn't need refrigeration, toasting, or your bullshit.

- You could eat them toasted, cold, crushed at the bottom of your Jansport, or two weeks expired — and they still slapped.

- The frosting? Sometimes a full coat of sugar armor. Sometimes a half-assed streak like someone sneezed a line of icing across the top and called it a day.

- The filling? **Molten fucking lava.** First bite burned your mouth, second bite burned your soul, third bite — pure nirvana.

- **Strawberry Frosted, Brown Sugar Cinnamon, S'mores** — the real ones knew.

- And those burnt edges? A rite of passage. Every toaster fucked them up. But we still showed up.

Pop-Tarts weren't just breakfast. They were **survival food** for the emotionally neglected and perpetually late. No one ever lovingly handed you a Pop-Tart — you grabbed that box yourself like a feral gremlin and shoved it in your face while searching for a clean sock.

TOASTER STRUDEL: THE BOUGIE BITCH

Then came Toaster Strudel. Soft. Fancy. Imported. Delicate. The golden child of the frozen breakfast aisle.

- Required actual adulting: a perfect toast, a delicate icing swirl, no room for chaos.

- That icing packet? A flex. You were suddenly an artist. A pastry surgeon.

- It smelled like rich people. Like your parents didn't fight over bills and your house had carpet that didn't crunch when you walked on it.

Toaster Strudel was flaky, soft, and beautiful — but it was high-maintenance. You couldn't just grab it and go. You had to babysit it. You had to earn it. And some mornings, **fuck that**.

THE VERDICT?

Toaster Strudel was a vibe — but Pop-Tarts were the fucking culture.

Pop-Tarts didn't care how tired you were.

They didn't ask for effort, they just showed up — like a sugar-coated middle finger to breakfast norms.

You could burn them, drop them, forget them in your backpack for three days and they still got the job done.

They were dependable, chaotic, and gloriously unhealthy.

Toaster Strudel might have looked like it had its shit together...

But Pop-Tarts *were* the shit.

LUNCHBOX HIERARCHY: WHO RULED THE CAFETERIA

Lunch at school wasn't about nutrition. It was about *clout*. Your lunchbox contents told the world who you were.

- **Lunchables**: The holy grail. You weren't eating lunch. You were *assembling* lunch like a tiny Gordon Ramsay. Bonus points for pizza or taco Lunchables.

- **Thermos Crew**: Some kids brought soup. Others brought Chef Boyardee ravioli in a dented thermos that smelled like nuclear tomatoes. Respect.

- **Sandwiches**: Always squished. Always questionable. PB&J was the gold standard. Bologna was a war crime.

- **Fruit Roll-Ups & Fruit by the Foot**: Dental napalm. Stuck in your molars until Christmas. But so worth it.

- **Capri Sun**: If you could actually get the straw in without stabbing through the back, you were a goddamn surgeon.

SNACK TIME WAS A BLOODSPORT

We didn't have "snack breaks." We had *feeding frenzies*.

- **Dunkaroos**: Animal crackers you dipped into icing with reckless abandon. The ultimate sugar-to-carb ratio.

- **Gushers**: Fruit snacks that exploded in your mouth like edible zits. Everyone wanted them. Nobody knew what they were.

- **Fruit Snacks**: Everything from Shark Bites to Scooby Snacks. They were barely food, but we pretended they were fruit so we didn't feel guilty.

- **Handi-Snacks**: Cheese so synthetic it should've come with a battery, spread with a red plastic spatula that looked like a murder weapon.

- **Yoplait Trix Yogurt**: Not food. Just neon slime disguised as dairy.

THE DRINKS THAT RAISED US (AND POSSIBLY POISONED US)

ECTO COOLER

This was the holy nectar of the 90s. Slimer-green and vaguely citrus-flavored, Ecto Cooler was a tie-in to *Ghostbusters* that outlasted its source material because it was that good. It was lunchbox currency. If you had it, you could trade for anything short of a Game Boy.

CRYSTAL PEPSI (THE MESSIAH OF SODAS)

Let's get this straight: **Crystal Pepsi wasn't a failure** — it was *ahead of its time.* It was futuristic. Revolutionary. Liquid rebellion in a clear bottle. It tasted like hope, purity, and just a whisper of cola. And if you didn't think it was elite, that's a *you* problem.

That commercial? The one with **Van Halen's "Right Now"** blaring while slow-mo shots of people doing epic shit played across the screen? That was our *national anthem.* That ad felt like it could end wars and cure seasonal depression.

When Crystal Pepsi vanished, it wasn't just discontinued — it *ascended.* And I've been waiting for its second coming ever since. Jesus might come back first, but I still keep one eye on the soda aisle just in case.

MOUNTAIN DEW (RISE OF THE XTREME)

Dew wasn't just a drink. It was a *lifestyle.* If you weren't BASE jumping while skateboarding down an active volcano after slamming a Dew, were you even living? This was the era when Mountain Dew realized its target audience was sleep-deprived teens playing GoldenEye at 3AM.

SNAPPLE & NANTUCKET NECTARS

These were your mom's way of feeling fancy. Snapple gave us "Real Facts" under the cap and flavors like Peach Tea that made you feel like you were part of a book club. Nantucket Nectars was Snapple's smoother cousin that showed up with a guitar and a flannel shirt. Both were early signs you were transitioning into your teen angst era.

SPRITE AND HIP-HOP

Sprite pulled one of the biggest power moves in marketing history. While Pepsi was busy trying to make Britney and Beyoncé sip a cola, Sprite said "nah" and went full *hip-hop*.

- Ads featured legends like KRS-One, A Tribe Called Quest, Nas, and Rakim.

- "Obey Your Thirst" wasn't just a slogan — it was a cultural moment.

Sprite became *the* drink for rap fans. It was crisp, cool, and came with street cred. This wasn't your dad's 7Up. This was the drink you sipped while freestyling in your driveway or bumping *Illmatic* from your Discman.

DESSERTS, DELIRIUM, AND DIABEETUS

- **Ninja Turtle Pies**: Green. Oozing with vanilla pudding. Created by a mad scientist or a marketing team on LSD. But they *slapped*.

- **Jell-O Pudding Pops**: Ice cream's cheap cousin. Came in weirdly swirled flavors and always left a film in your mouth.

- **Push Pops & Ring Pops**: Candy disguised as fashion. Sticky, messy, and a choking hazard if you tried to bite through them (which we all did).

- **Choco Tacos**: The pinnacle of frozen innovation. A taco shell made of waffle cone and filled with ice cream? Genius.

FAST FOOD MANIA AND COMMERCIAL BRAINWASHING

We were groomed by jingles.

- **"Pizza in the morning, pizza in the evening..."** Bagel Bites made it okay to eat pizza 24/7.

- **Hot Pockets**: Molten lava inside a cardboard shell. Risk of third-degree burns: 100%.

- **McDonald's**: Happy Meals, playgrounds, and collectibles. That Monopoly game? A rigged dream. But we still believed.

- **Taco Bell**: The 59¢/79¢/99¢ menu let you ball out on $3.

- **Pizza Hut**: Home of the Book-It Program and personal pan pizzas that made you feel like a scholar *and* a baller.

EXPERIMENTAL FOOD FAILS (AND WE LOVED THEM ANYWAY)

- **Orbitz**: A drink with floating balls. Looked like a lava lamp. Tasted like bad decisions.

- **Green Ketchup**: Heinz went full Joker-mode. Gross, but we all tried it.

- **Squeezits**: Plastic bottle you crushed while chugging sugary dye. Squeezing it made it taste better. Science.

- **Olestra**: The chip additive that literally warned of "anal leakage" and somehow still got approved. You could eat more chips... but at what cost?

FINAL BITES: HOW WE ATE, WHY WE REMEMBER

We were the experimental batch. The beta testers for modern junk food. No nutrition labels. No sugar warnings. No apps telling us how many steps we needed to burn off a single Dunkaroo. We just *ate*.

Our childhood was a buffet of chaos: food that was barely real, drinks that glowed, and snacks that probably knocked five years off our lifespan - but every single bite, sip, and crunch was worth it. And through it all, we bonded. Over pizza bagels. Over trading snacks at lunch. Over a single pouch of Ecto Cooler that made you the king of the playground.

Gen X didn't just snack. We *survived* on flavor. On friendship. And on questionable FDA oversight.

Welcome to our food pyramid. It's shaped like a Lunchable, and it's collapsing under the weight of 90s excellence.

OUR REAL PARENTS WERE TELEVISION & TRAUMA

Y ou want to know who raised Gen X? It wasn't just Mom and Dad. Hell, half the time they were at work, divorced, or passed out on the couch after a long day of surviving Reaganomics. **Our third parent was the TV.** A glowing box of chaos, comfort, and confusion that babysat us, educated us, terrified us, and occasionally made us question reality itself.

This chapter isn't just a look at the shows we watched. It's a **full-blown, unapologetic autopsy** of the cultural content that molded our personalities, warped our attention spans, and injected us with sarcasm, distrust, and an oddly passionate understanding of stranger danger. You want wholesome? Go read a Highlights magazine. This is the *real* shit.

We weren't passive viewers. We were *disciples.* We memorized theme songs like scripture. We lined up for Saturday morning cartoons like it was church. We took in PSAs from cartoons that doubled as war propaganda and ate up sugary morality tales disguised as "very special episodes." Our sitcoms came with trauma, our cartoons came with consumerism, and our after-school programming occasionally included satanic panic exposés.

This chapter is massive because it has to be. There's no short way to explain what TV meant to Gen X. **It was everything.** It shaped how we saw the world, how we treated each other, how we handled grief, how we cracked jokes. We were raised by Blanche Devereaux, Uncle Jesse, Optimus Prime, and that bastard Robert Stack whispering ghost stories into our souls. We were emotionally manipulated by NBC bumpers and had our worldview shattered by *Unsolved Mysteries* at 8 years old.

We didn't have tablets. We had one TV in the living room, and if your older sibling wanted to watch *90210*, you just had to shut up and learn about Brenda's trauma. If your dad was watching *Cheers*, then guess what, you suddenly had an honorary degree in alcoholism and loneliness by age 10.

This chapter is your time machine. It's your mixtape. It's the screaming intro to your favorite show and the comforting static of a late-night signoff. It's the Kool-Aid Man wrecking your kitchen and the Schoolhouse Rock song you can still sing *word for word* while blackout drunk.

Welcome to the chapter that raised us.

Don't skip the intro...

~ 5 ~

TV AND GEN X

Television wasn't just background noise for Gen X kids. It was a babysitter, a teacher, a moral compass, and occasionally, the reason we had nightmares or asked weird questions in class. We didn't have a thousand channels or 24/7 streaming. We had to work with rabbit ears, dial knobs, and maybe a top-loading VCR that weighed more than we did. But man, what we had? It was pure magic. Unfiltered, weird, chaotic, and somehow comforting. Like a fever dream you didn't know you needed.

SATURDAY MORNING CARTOONS: OUR SACRED WEEKLY RITUAL

If you were a Gen X kid, Saturday morning wasn't just another day—it was THE day. The only reason we willingly set an alarm on the weekend. Saturday mornings were the reward for surviving five days of school lunches, dodgeball bruises, and being told to go play outside until the streetlights came on. This was our holy time.

You rolled out of bed, feet hitting the cold linoleum floor, still half-asleep but already dreaming of the technicolor mind-melt that was waiting in the living room. A bowl of knockoff cereal in hand (unless you were bougie enough for Lucky Charms or Cookie Crisp), you'd plop yourself down in front of the TV and let the glow raise you better than any babysitter ever could.

There were only three networks really in the game: ABC, CBS, and NBC. That's it. No Nickelodeon, no Cartoon Network, no Net-flix Kids with parental controls. Just three monolithic networks at war with each other for our sugar-fueled attention spans. Each one had a tight 4–5 hour block of cartoons. And it wasn't just the shows—it was the scheduling strategy. You flipped back and forth like a maniac if *Teenage Mutant Ninja Turtles* on CBS was airing dur-ing *Pee-wee's Playhouse* on CBS. It was serious business. You had to be quick. You had to prioritize. This was your Saturday stock port-folio.

These blocks were anchored by giants:

- *He-Man and the Masters of the Universe*: Sword-wielding, jacked to the gods, screaming about Grayskull. Skeletor had better insults than half the internet.

- *She-Ra: Princess of Power*: She wasn't a sidekick. She was a full-on warrior queen, out here defending Etheria and breaking gender norms with every glittery transformation.

- *Thundercats*: Cats with abs and weapons and existential monologues. You didn't just watch *Thundercats*—you spiritu-ally trained for it.

- *The Smurfs*: Blue, communist-adjacent mushroom dwellers with an unclear breeding system. The first world-building franchise you ever encountered.

- *The Real Ghostbusters*: They had proton packs and a green blob named Slimer. These were your actual heroes, not the

B-movie knockoff ones with the talking gorilla.

- *Muppet Babies*: This show *shaped* our imaginations. Full-on parodying movies like *Star Wars* and *Indiana Jones*, with licensed footage and everything.

- *Dungeons & Dragons*: This was an honest-to-god dark fantasy epic hidden in the cartoon block. These kids were trapped. They never got home. The unicorn cried. We cried.

- *Gummi Bears*: If you didn't pretend to drink Gummiberry Juice and bounce off walls, you wasted your childhood.

- *Pee-wee's Playhouse*: A chaotic, technicolor variety fever dream with talking furniture, secret words, and Laurence Fishburne as Cowboy Curtis. This was postmodernism before we knew the word.

- *The Bugs Bunny and Tweety Show*: The glue that bound our grandparents to us. Looney Tunes reruns were the bridge between generations. Wile E. Coyote was our tragic antihero.

Let's not forget the real weirdos:

- *Rubik the Amazing Cube*: He floated. He talked. He was a cursed object and no one ever questioned it.

- *The Littles*: Human-adjacent mouse people with tails who lived in walls and fixed your lights. Totally normal.

- *Turbo Teen*: A teenage boy turns into a car when he gets hot. I don't know what the writers were on, but bless them for this nightmare.

- *Hulk Hogan's Rock 'n' Wrestling*: It somehow made actual wrestling *less* believable.

Commercial breaks weren't breaks. They were RECRUITMENT SESSIONS. We sat up straight. We paid attention. These were our calls to action.

- *My Buddy and Kid Sister*: "Wherever I go, he goes!" Yeah, straight into the uncanny valley.

- *Skip-It*: The toy designed to destroy ankles.

- *Crossfire*: If you didn't scream "YOU'LL GET CAUGHT UP IN THE CROSSFIRE" with the music, were you even alive?

- *Lite Brite, Creepy Crawlers, Madballs, Stretch Armstrong, Pogo Balls, Popples, Pound Puppies*—the entire catalog of 80s toy marketing gold lived here.

And then the PSAs. God-tier weirdness mixed with actual life lessons. This was how we learned:

- *Time for Timer*: A talking meatball with limbs reminding you to eat string cheese?

- *Schoolhouse Rock*: These weren't jingles. These were *national treasures*. "Conjunction Junction" still slaps.

- *The More You Know*: These star-streak animations would drop knowledge like, "Don't light your little brother on fire, Jeremy."

- *G.I. Joe*: Every episode ended with some scenario that had *nothing* to do with the plot. "Don't talk to strangers. Now you know!" "And knowing is half the battle."

- *Smokey the Bear*: That solemn, haunting stare. "Only YOU..." made you feel like you already committed the arson.

This wasn't just TV. This was tribal memory. Shared language. You showed up to school on Monday quoting lines, humming themes, reenacting fights. Saturday morning cartoons built our social capital.

And when it ended? Around 11 or noon, you'd go outside and become what you watched. Capes made out of pillowcases. Sticks became swords. Bikes turned into Battle Cats. You weren't just playing. You were *continuing the narrative.*

Future generations will never understand this ecosystem. They'll never know the anxiety of choosing between two bangers airing at the same time. Or the heartbreak of missing an episode and having to *wait a full year* for a possible rerun. They won't know the high of seeing a new toy commercial drop and realizing that your birthday list just got rewritten.

Saturday morning wasn't about zoning out. It was about *tuning in.* Deeply. Wildly. Passionately. It was a ritual. A gathering. A joy only the feral chaos of Gen X could truly appreciate.

And then came the emotional carpet bomb that was *Transformers: The Movie* (1986). Hasbro looked at a generation of loyal, bright-eyed children and basically said, "You like Optimus Prime? That's cute. Watch him die." That movie was an ambush. Nobody warned us. No one prepared us. You walked into that theater expecting robot battles and walked out a broken shell of your former self. Optimus didn't just die, he *flatlined* on a steel table in full cinematic drama, eyes going dim as he handed over the Matrix of Leadership. That scene didn't just hit, it *haunted*. Kids cried in the aisles. Some didn't speak for days. Parents wrote angry letters.

Why? Because Hasbro had toys to sell. New toys. New characters. So they cleaned house in the most traumatic way possible. Ironhide? Dead. Prowl? Dead. Ratchet? Dead. Wheeljack? DEAD. You barely had time to process one loss before another beloved Autobot got smoked. Enter Rodimus Prime, Springer, Arcee, Ultra Magnus—and we were just supposed to go along with it like our childhood wasn't actively on fire. Hasbro took the Saturday morning loyalty we gave them and turned it into a business strategy soaked in the tears of ten-year-olds. It was brutal. It was effective. And decades later, we're still unpacking it in therapy.

Like, let's be real here: for the entire run of the *Transformers* cartoon, nobody could hit anything. Autobots and Decepticons spent whole episodes shooting lasers in wild directions while quipping and ducking behind rocks. The only thing consistently injured were background buildings and your patience. But five minutes into this feature-length trauma bomb, this paid trigger warning without the actual warning, and the Decepticons suddenly got deadly as hell. It was like Megatron and crew went off to train with Seal Team 6 in the offseason and came back with bloodlust and headshots. Ironhide didn't even get a last line. He got *clapped*. Wheeljack was dead *off-screen*. Like, damn. Did we do something to deserve this?

But here's the kicker: that soundtrack SLAPS. "The Touch" by Stan Bush? Still a banger. "Dare"? Eternal. That movie might've wrecked us emotionally, but it also gave us one of the most metal animated soundtracks of all time. So yeah, Hasbro chose violence, but they also gave us something unforgettable. Thanks, I guess?

So yes, Saturday morning was our weekly revival. It was where chaos reigned, heroes were born, and friendships were forged over the debate of who was stronger, Lion-O or He-Man. And if you're a Gen Xer reading this, I already know the answer lives deep in your bones.

WEEKDAY AFTER-SCHOOL TV: THE SECOND SHIFT OF OUR EDUCATION

If Saturday mornings were sacred, then weekday afternoons were straight-up lawless. This was when the school day ended, the backpack hit the floor with a thud, and the TV went *click* before you even got your shoes off. Your parents were still at work. You were unsupervised. And the glow of the cathode ray tube was your portal to chaos, comedy, and cartoons that ran on sugar and adrenaline.

Let's start with *The Disney Afternoon* block. That was like getting the deluxe Happy Meal of cartoons every single weekday. You had:

- *DuckTales*: Scrooge McDuck swimming in gold coins, risking child endangerment charges daily. That theme song alone could bring a grown Gen Xer to tears.

- *Chip 'n Dale: Rescue Rangers*: Rodent vigilantes solving crimes while dressed like Magnum P.I. and Indiana Jones. No notes. Perfect show.

- *TailSpin*: A reimagining of *The Jungle Book* as a sky pirate action series. Yes, Baloo was an airline pilot. And yes, we just accepted that.

- *Darkwing Duck*: A vigilante duck with a gas gun and a flair for the dramatic. Batman wishes he had this much sauce.

And before Disney bought everything that breathed, there was *Voltron*, *Robotech*, *MASK*, and *Inspector Gadget*. Syndicated shows you had to catch at the *exact* right time or risk being lost in the story forever. There was no pause button. There were no recaps. If Penny figured something out and you missed it? Tough. Good luck following next week's plot.

You also had the weird, wild experiments, those shows that felt like someone pitched them after a fever dream and they somehow got greenlit:

- *Camp Candy*: John Candy as a cartoon camp counselor. Half heartfelt, half chaos.

- *Beetlejuice*: Based on the movie, but somehow darker, weirder, and 100% more unhinged.

- *Attack of the Killer Tomatoes*: Yes, based on the movie about homicidal produce. And yes, it got a full animated series run. Because why the hell not?

- *Bobby's World*: Howie Mandel voicing a big-headed kid in a weird Midwestern purgatory. Strangely relatable.

Then came the live-action oddities:

- *Punky Brewster*: Half after-school special, half comedy, 100% iconic. Punky power was real. She had mismatched shoes, a treehouse in the apartment courtyard, and a dog named Brandon with more charisma than half the cast of *Friends*. But it wasn't all fun and scrunchies. One episode had Punky get locked in an abandoned refrigerator while playing hide and seek—an episode that scarred an entire generation and made us scared of discarded appliances for life. And who can forget the storyline where Cherie nearly suffocates in that same fridge? That wasn't a sitcom moment. That was a trauma bond.

- *Small Wonder*: A robot girl pretending to be a regular child. The acting was robotic. On purpose? Debatable. Vicki (the robot) had zero facial expressions and delivered lines like HAL 9000 doing community theater. But somehow, it worked. She was a walking lie detector, a babysitter with superhuman strength, and a one-girl commentary on suburban dysfunction. The show tried to teach lessons about honesty and fairness through a CGI-blinking robot, and we all bought in because we had no other context for what normal looked like.

- *Out of This World*: A teenage girl with the power to freeze time. The intro song alone was a spiritual experience. Evie Garland could touch her fingers together and instantly pause the universe. What did she use this omnipotent power for? Mostly petty drama, avoiding chores, and teen angst.

Her dad was an alien who communicated with her via a glowing cube voiced by Burt Reynolds, because why the hell not? One episode had her clone herself to do chores, and the clone turned evil. It was a cosmic warning against laziness that doubled as low-budget sci-fi horror.

- *Alf*: An alien living with a suburban family who eats cats. This was *prime time* content but reran after school. Which is how Gen X kids learned sarcasm. Alf was rude, nosy, always hungry, and somehow still more emotionally honest than most humans. There was a whole subplot where Alf tried to build a spaceship in the garage while hiding from the government. Another episode had him dealing with survivor's guilt over his planet's destruction. ALF was dark comedy wrapped in a puppet and served with a side of cat jokes. And it worked.

And then there was the strange phenomenon of Rated R movies getting Saturday morning or after-school cartoon spin-offs. Like, full-on, no shame, here's a cartoon for children based on a film your parents weren't even sure *they* should've watched. *Rambo: The Force of Freedom* was a thing. A *real thing*. They took one of the most violent, PTSD-soaked action franchises ever made and said, "Let's put this war machine in a cartoon with a bunch of toy-ready sidekicks." And we loved it. Didn't even blink.

Then came *RoboCop: The Animated Series*. The same RoboCop who got his hand and brain blown out in the most disturbing opening scene of all time? Yup, now he had a Saturday morning cartoon—and a matching lunchbox. There were *Toxic Crusaders*, based on *The Toxic Avenger*, a Troma film filled with gore and nudity. The cartoon dialed it back and gave the lead mutant a conscience. Sure. Makes total sense.

They even tried to launch a *Police Academy* cartoon. You know, from the movie with language, nudity, and adult gags that 8-year-olds absolutely should not be quoting—but we did anyway. And *Conan the Adventurer*? The man who chopped heads and had orgies in the movies? Now toned down into a kid-friendly sword-wielder fighting snake cults with morals at the end.

These weren't just cartoons—they were gateway drugs into movie franchises we absolutely had no business watching, but somehow we *did*. Because the 80s and 90s didn't care about age ratings. They cared about action figures, and if that meant putting Rambo on the shelf next to He-Man, so be it. We were sold violence in pastel colors with a catchy theme song, and it absolutely worked on us.

After-school programming wasn't just escapism. It was a chance to breathe. To laugh. To decompress from being force-fed math facts and overhead projector transparencies all day. It was your reward for surviving spelling tests and suspicious cafeteria meat.

It's where the foundation of your pop culture memory was poured. You memorized theme songs like scripture. You learned life lessons wrapped in fart jokes. And every once in a while, a Very Special Episode slipped in and hit you with some heavy truth before dinner. This was our second shift of education, and we took it *very* seriously.

And we haven't even gotten to the game shows, SNICK, or Nickelodeon yet. Buckle up. It only gets wilder from here.

SECTION 3: PSAS, EDUCATIONAL WEIRDNESS, AND LOW-KEY NIGHTMARES

In between all the cartoons, sitcoms, and puppet-fueled chaos, Gen X kids got hit with bursts of moral guidance so intense they should've come with therapy vouchers. I'm talking about those Public Service Announcements (PSAs), bumpers, and weirdly captivating educational interludes that were crammed into our programming like spinach in a brownie. You didn't ask for it—but you ate it anyway.

First off, let's talk about Schoolhouse Rock. If you were a Gen X kid, this wasn't just some background jingle nonsense, this was foundational curriculum. These short interludes didn't just teach, they slapped. They were the original micro-learning. They got in, dropped a funky beat about nouns or taxes, and dipped out like pros.

Let's break it down:

- Grammar Rock: "Conjunction Junction" taught us how to link thoughts together long before we could spell half the words we were using. "Lolly, Lolly, Lolly, Get Your Adverbs Here" was three generations of adverb-pushers in one catchy tune. "Interjections!" showed us it was perfectly fine to scream "Hey!" or "Ow!" in a sentence, as long as it had an exclamation point.

- America Rock: "I'm Just a Bill" is arguably more responsible for kids understanding the U.S. legislative process than any civics textbook ever written. That poor bill sitting on the steps of Capitol Hill? The struggle was real. "The Preamble" put the Constitution to music and somehow made it memorable enough that we can still recite it, backed by a gospel choir in our heads—decades later. "No More Kings" made the American Revolution seem like a breakup anthem. "The Shot Heard Round the World" turned Lexington and Concord into straight-up battle bars.

- Multiplication Rock: You didn't know math until "Three is a Magic Number" whispered it into your soul. "My Hero, Zero," "The Four-Legged Zoo," and "Figure Eight" all took dry math facts and spun them into psychedelic singalongs. "Naughty Number Nine" made multiplication sound like noir jazz. Honestly, how the hell did they make this stuff so cool?

- Science Rock: "Electricity, Electricity!" turned physics into funk. "Telegraph Line" was a melancholy banger about communication technology. "Them Not-So-Dry Bones" taught anatomy with creepy, spooky energy. And "A Victim of Gravity" explained physics using doo-wop harmonies that rivaled The Platters.

- Money Rock: This one came a little later, but it went hard. "Tyrannosaurus Debt" used a dinosaur metaphor to explain the national debt. "This for That" broke down bartering. "Where the Money Goes" actually explained taxes to kids. And yes, it was still somehow catchy.

What made Schoolhouse Rock so effective was the animation style, the groovy-yet-dorky singers, and the fact that it never talked down to kids. These weren't nursery rhymes. These were lessons, wrapped in funk, jazz, soul, and pop arrangements with vocalists who sounded like they were really feeling these multiplication tables.

You didn't just watch Schoolhouse Rock. You memorized it. You sang along. You accidentally learned something before your cereal even got soggy. And when your teacher busted out a pop quiz on grammar, history, or fractions? Boom...your brain queued up a melody and saved your ass.

It wasn't just content—it was cultural glue. It made education cool without trying too hard. And to this day, if someone starts singing "I'm just a bill..." you know the next line. Doesn't matter if you're 8 or 48. That's power.

Then came the mini-legends: Time for Timer and Yuck Mouth. Timer was that strange clock-shaped creature who screamed about snacks, string cheese, and brushing your teeth in a cowboy accent while bouncing around like he was on something stronger than Vitamin C. Meanwhile, Yuck Mouth was a crusty, food-covered, bad-breath gremlin who existed to shame you into flossing. Honestly? He succeeded. No kid wanted to become a crust punk cavity case with teeth that looked like abandoned buildings.

But it wasn't just the silly stuff. The PSAs meant business. "The More You Know" with that now-iconic shooting star and synth chime was NBC's way of getting celebrities to drop little nuggets of truth—everything from "Don't lie to your parents" to "Don't play in refrigerators." It was quick, punchy, and just vague enough to haunt your dreams.

One to Grow On took it a step further. Stars from shows like Diff'rent Strokes, Silver Spoons, and Family Ties would pop out of character mid-episode to talk to you about shoplifting, peer pressure, or lying. Imagine Jason Bateman looking you in the eye to tell you stealing gum is a gateway to prison. That was the vibe.

Then came the drug PSAs—the apex of 80s fear-based marketing. The egg-in-the-frying-pan commercial is burned into every Gen Xer's brain. "This is your brain... This is your brain on drugs... Any questions?" Yeah. We had a lot. Like, "Why is this more terrifying than Freddy Krueger?" And there were dozens more:

- The girl smashing up a kitchen to prove what addiction does to your family.

- The dad interrogating his son, only for the kid to yell, "I learned it by watching YOU!"

- The animated one where a cartoon dog raps about cocaine addiction with his human friend and somehow ends up crying.

No one was safe from the message. Not even our cartoons. Cartoon All-Stars to the Rescue was the god-tier crossover event nobody asked for and everybody saw. Garfield, Bugs Bunny, ALF, the Muppet Babies, the Smurfs, and the Ninja Turtles all teamed up like the Avengers to stage a drug intervention for a teenager spiraling into reefer madness. They went full multiverse, busting through walls, hallucinations, and musical numbers just to say: "Put the joint down, kid."

And we haven't even talked about GI Joe yet. Every episode ended with some kid lighting a grill next to a propane tank or trying to swim during a lightning storm, and out popped a Joe character to deliver a life-saving lesson in thirty seconds flat. "Don't talk to strangers." "Don't mix household chemicals." "Wear life vests." The response was always the same: "Now I know." And the reply? The line Gen X took to the grave: "And knowing is half the battle!"

We also had Smokey Bear, who was dead serious and gave no room for bullshit. "Only YOU can prevent forest fires." He said it like he knew you were already plotting to play with matches. And McGruff the Crime Dog? He wanted you to "Take a bite out of crime," but his gritty detective voice made it feel like you were watching a wiretap in a D.A.R.E. sting.

There were also deep-cut horrors like Stranger Danger videos, where you'd watch child actors get lured into vans or nearly abducted in parking lots. These segments aired on random afternoons with all the subtlety of a Law & Order: SVU episode, leaving you convinced every ice cream truck was a trap.

And don't forget the environmental PSAs. Captain Planet tried his best, but sometimes it was those in-between bumpers—the ones that said "Don't litter" or "Turn off the faucet" that really made you stop and think, "Am I killing the planet by brushing my teeth for too long?"

All of this was squeezed between commercials for sugar cereal and violent toy commercials. It was emotional whiplash. One minute you're watching Michelangelo surf a sewer pipe, and the next you're being guilt-tripped about nuclear fallout and cigarette butts.

Gen X didn't have therapy. We had Mr. Rogers reminding us we were special, a talking clock warning us about blood sugar crashes, and cartoon turtles begging us not to smoke weed. We were raised on jingles and fear, love and trauma, logic and lunacy, all cut together in 30-second bursts that played between a cartoon about alien cats and a commercial for Crossfire.

It was weird. It was unsettling. It was unforgettable. And honestly? It worked.

SECTION 4: PRIMETIME SITCOMS AND DRAMA BOMBS – OUR UNOFFICIAL LIFE COACHES

Primetime TV in the Gen X era wasn't just entertainment, it was a crash course in life, love, trauma, sarcasm, and how to survive in a world where your dad was too tired to talk and your mom was chain-smoking her way through dinner. This was the real school. We sat in front of that box every night like disciples at the Church of Must-See TV. These shows didn't just raise us. They cracked us open, dumped a mix of laughter, awkward hugs, generational baggage, and deep-rooted emotional issues inside, and called it parenting.

Let's kick this off with the family sitcoms that smiled in your face while slipping a moral lesson in your back pocket:

- Family Ties: The Keatons were a walking identity crisis. Hippie parents raising a Reagan-worshipping son? That was peak generational whiplash. Alex P. Keaton was out here quoting Adam Smith at the breakfast table while Mallory just wanted to curl her bangs. It was capitalism vs. free love, and somehow it all wrapped up with a life lesson and a freeze-frame hug by the credits.

- Growing Pains: Dr. Jason Seaver ran a full-time therapy practice out of his house while trying to keep Mike Seaver from becoming a full-blown menace. Kirk Cameron was the charming troublemaker with a punchable smirk, and yet you still rooted for him. Every week, Mike did something dumb, Carol lectured him, Ben was ignored, and by the end—boom, everything was fixed because Dad hit you with a tender, echoey monologue and a single tear. Cue soft music.

• The Cosby Show: Look, we know how things turned out, but in its moment, this was top-tier Black excellence. Cliff Huxtable in wild sweaters eating hoagies in the middle of a jazz solo? Iconic. Claire was the attorney mom we all feared and adored. Theo was dumb in the most lovable way possible. And the Gordon Gartrell shirt? That was a rite of passage. It showed you what family could be when it was loud, loving, and brutally honest.

• Full House: Danny Tanner was cleaning like he was about to summon a demon if there was a single speck of dust. Uncle Jesse had a mullet that should've had its own SAG card. And Joey? Joey was just... there. Telling Popeye impressions and probably smelling like microwave burritos. But those piano-backed speeches at the end? Those hit. And don't act like you didn't try to pull off a "You got it, dude!" at some point and fail miserably.

• Silver Spoons: Rich kid wish-fulfillment. Ricky literally had a damn train in his house. A TRAIN. And still had the audacity to complain about anything. The only thing more unrealistic than his living room theme park was how emotionally available his dad was.

• Who's the Boss?: A Brooklyn ex-ballplayer becomes a live-in housekeeper for an uptight executive woman, and all the sexual tension gets bottlenecked into seven seasons of "will-they-won't-they" stares and awkward hallway moments. Mona was out here smashing the patriarchy—and probably the delivery guy. Angela had shoulder pads that could deflect bullets, and Tony vacuumed in sweatpants like it was foreplay.

Now to the "kid gets adopted by white people and we pretend this is normal" subgenre:

- Diff'rent Strokes: You can't tell me Arnold Drummond wasn't a comedic genius. His timing? Impeccable. But that bike shop episode? Oh, that was a tone shift. That was the moment childhood cracked a little. You went from laughing at Willis to realizing the world had teeth.

- Webster: Emmanuel Lewis had charm levels so high they had to write entire episodes around him just giving a look. He could break your heart with a head tilt. Also, Webster falling into those gaps in the staircase? It was both comedy gold and an OSHA violation.

- Punky Brewster: She had the energy of a punk band lead singer and the trauma of a Lifetime movie protagonist. She turned abandonment into personality. Her room looked like Lisa Frank's fever dream, but her emotional depth? Whew. Punky gave us scrunchie-wrapped strength. And when she went through the Challenger tragedy in an episode? The writers held nothing back. Not a damn thing.

Then came the anti-sitcoms. The real ones. The ones that said, "Nah, we're not wrapping this up neatly."

- Married... with Children: This show was straight-up therapy for people who grew up yelling over dinner. Al Bundy was a man defeated by life but still too stubborn to die. He hated everything. His job. His house. His shoes. His kids. Peg was a goddess of glam-trash who made laziness look iconic. Kelly was hot and dumb, and Bud was short and horny. And none of them gave a damn about your feelings.

- Roseanne: This was the Midwestern truth bomb. The Connors were broke, bitter, tired, and realer than anything we'd ever seen. They fought like your parents did. They laughed like they needed to. Dan was the TV dad who didn't give speeches—he just hugged you and hoped for the best. And when this show got heavy, it got heavy. From domestic abuse to birth control to mental health, Roseanne pulled zero punches.

- The Wonder Years: Kevin Arnold was everyone's inner monologue. That show gave us longing and regret before we knew what those words meant. Winnie Cooper wasn't just a crush—she was the crush. Daniel Stern's voiceover could take a kid dropping his ice cream and make it feel like a metaphor for mortality. And that soundtrack? That wasn't music—it was emotional manipulation.

Deep cuts? We had 'em too:

- Mr. Belvedere: British butler raising an American family with sass and side-eyes. He kept that house running better than the parents did.

- Perfect Strangers: Balki Bartokomous was pure chaos with a heart of gold. Cousin Larry was all anxiety and cheap suits. Together? Sitcom gold.

- Head of the Class, Just the Ten of Us, My Two Dads—they all got their moment. Some were great. Some were weird. But they were ours.

Primetime was the time you learned how to exist. How to deal. How to hurt and laugh in the same breath. These shows weren't just stories, they were roadmaps. They were warm blankets and cautionary tales. They were flawed families teaching us that it was okay to be a little broken.

And just when things started to feel safe, like maybe you were gonna coast into bedtime on a cloud of chuckles and nostalgia—a Very Special Episode would roll up, tap you on the shoulder, and whisper, "Not tonight, kid. Tonight, you feel shit." But we'll get there soon enough.

SECTION 5: THE VERY SPECIAL EPISODE – WHEN TV PUNCHED US IN THE SOUL

Let's not sugarcoat it. The Very Special Episode was a genre all its own. These weren't just regular episodes of your favorite show. No. These were full-on televised trauma dumps disguised as family entertainment. They came out of nowhere, unannounced, with no trigger warning, no prep, no safe word, just a cold open and a vibe that told you something was off. You started the episode expecting a laugh track and ended up rethinking your entire life while hugging a pillow and staring into the void.

You remember the signs: the music was slower, the jokes stopped landing, and the lighting dimmed like the director knew, "Yeah, we're about to wreck some childhoods tonight."

Let's start where the trauma tree was planted: Diff'rent Strokes.

There are a lot of Very Special Episodes out there, but none...and I mean NONE...came harder than the bike shop episode. Arnold and Dudley meet a charming shop owner named Mr. Horton. He gives them free bike parts, soda, cartoons... and then hits us with the old "backroom photo session" setup. This man was a full-on predator, and the show didn't pull a single damn punch. He got Dudley drunk, showed him dirty cartoons, and tried to lure Arnold into a bath. You could feel the studio audience squirming. No laughs. Just dread. Just a slow descent into what-the-fuck-is-happening territory. And here's the wild part...this was still played in syndication for years. Gen X got baptized in uncomfortable truth like it was part of the Saturday morning cartoon lineup.

Punky Brewster said, "Hold my rainbow suspenders." Let's talk about the fridge. Cherie gets stuck in an old discarded refrigerator while playing hide-and-seek. She suffocates. Like, clinically. And Punky finds her unconscious. This wasn't just a PSA about appliance safety. This was full-on nightmare fuel. And they did not resolve it quickly. They let Punky panic. They let Henry scream. They made you sit in that terror. The fridge episode hit so hard that it spawned real-world legislation and school campaigns. That's right. Punky Brewster out here changing laws while we clutched our Cabbage Patch dolls in horror.

How about the Family Ties drunk driving episode? Alex's best friend Greg dies in a car crash. Not gets hurt. Dies. They show the grief. They show the guilt. And Alex loses it. It's just Michael J. Fox in a dark room, monologuing to an empty chair, asking why his friend isn't coming back. No music. No comfort. Just raw, uncut despair. The sitcom format collapsed under that weight, and it was glorious.

Then there's Saved by the Bell—the gateway drug to trauma that came in neon colors and freeze frames. Jessie Spano, high on caffeine pills, spiraling into academic meltdown: "I'm so excited! I'm so excited! I'm so... scared!" That line is etched into Gen X brain matter like a brand. It wasn't just about drugs. It was about the panic of trying to be perfect in a world that constantly demanded more. And she wasn't on heroin. She was on NO-DOZ. That's how raw it was—we were getting wrecked over legal stimulants.

The Fresh Prince of Bel-Air gave us one of the most emotionally devastating scenes in sitcom history when Will's dad walked out again. He turns to Uncle Phil, fists clenched, voice cracking, and hits us with: "How come he don't want me, man?" And Uncle Phil just holds him. That wasn't acting. That was therapy in real time. That scene didn't just sting—it detonated.

Even cartoons weren't safe. GI Joe ended every episode with a moral tip, but the episode about Shipwreck being trapped in a simulated future where his family dissolves before his eyes? That shit was dystopian. It was like Philip K. Dick took over the script room.

Full House once dropped a bomb when Stephanie finds out her classmate's dad is abusing him. This was not a laugh-track moment. It was dead serious. And it wasn't solved with a hug. It was solved with calling the cops. That episode taught us that sometimes, being a good friend meant breaking the silence. For a show that usually solved everything with a talk and some piano, this one hit.

And don't sleep on Boy Meets World. That show snuck in episodes on cults, grief, and abuse like it was just another Friday night. The cult episode where Shawn gets brainwashed into a new-age religion? Bro. That's Scientology-coded trauma delivered between Corey's one-liners. And then Mr. Turner gets into a motorcycle crash and disappears for the rest of the series. They didn't just write him off. They ghosted him. They trauma dumped and dipped.

Blossom hit teen pregnancy, addiction, parental abandonment, and abuse. One episode had Blossom's friend Six show up drunk at her house, breaking down into a panic attack. No joke, no tidy solution—just raw consequences.

Hell, even Dinosaurs, the show with puppets!!! Ended its run with an extinction-level ecological catastrophe. They let the Ice Age kill off the whole Sinclair family. No deus ex machina. No reset. Just global death. You watched your favorite dino family stare at the snow, knowing they were going to die. Goodnight, kids.

These episodes didn't just shape us, they scarred us in ways we're still unpacking. And yet... we watched. We sat through the whole thing. Because we knew—deep down—that sometimes life isn't fair. Sometimes it hurts. Sometimes your favorite characters cry, and sometimes they don't make it out okay.

TV in the Gen X era didn't coddle. It cracked knuckles and said, "Sit your ass down, this is gonna sting." And we respected it for that.

The Very Special Episode wasn't just a one-off. It was the moment when television stopped pretending—and started telling the
truth.

SECTION 6: GAME SHOW MAYHEM AND MESSY KID COMPETITIONS

Let's talk about the unhinged, beautifully chaotic universe of
Gen X game shows. These weren't your carefully scripted, slow-
moving quiz programs with some tie-wearing British guy whispering into a mic. No. These were battlefields of foam obstacles, trivia
panic, collapsing rope ladders, and a level of slime deployment
that would qualify as biochemical warfare by today's standards.

This was our coliseum. Our proving ground. Our only real shot
at immortality before the internet was a thing. We didn't want
scholarships. We wanted grossly oversized novelty checks and a
new Huffy.

First stop: the Nickelodeon Cinematic Universe, where dignity
went to die, and every surface was slippery.

- Double Dare: This was the Super Bowl of slop. The trivia
  didn't matter. No one ever remembered the questions. What
  mattered was the moment when someone shouted "PHYS-
  ICAL CHALLENGE!" and everything went to hell. Suddenly,
  kids were elbow-deep in a giant nose looking for a neon flag.
  They crawled through whipped cream, got pied in the face,
  and slid into a pool of what I'm convinced was expired Jell-O
  and dish soap. Marc Summers hosted this madness with the
  calm poise of a hostage negotiator. He wore khakis and a polite smile while children obliterated their childhoods in pud-

ding. Legend.

- Family Double Dare: Because why humiliate just kids when you can drag their parents into the nonsense? Watching your dad fall face-first into baked beans while your mom tried to balance a stack of sponges on her head? That's peak family bonding. Therapy in motion.

- GUTS: This show asked the hard question: what if kids had the Olympic Games, but every event looked like it was built by a manic toddler with a glue gun and a trampoline? Enter: The Aggro Crag. That glowing, fog-spewing mountain of doom that turned even the most coordinated child into a flailing mess. There were bungee races, inflatable obstacle courses, and water cannons fired with the subtlety of a riot squad. And Mo, the British referee? She was the only adult in the room. Respect her forever.

- Legends of the Hidden Temple: I will die on the hill that this was not a game show. This was a psychological thriller. You had to memorize a story about a cursed pineapple from the Mayan Empire, then answer questions, complete team relay challenges, and survive THE TEMPLE RUN. The Temple Run was where it all came crashing down. You could've been killing it all day and then freeze like a deer in headlights because you couldn't figure out how to assemble a three-piece monkey statue. And just when you thought you had it? BAM—temple guard. Gone. Snatched. Never seen again. Kids walked off this show with PTSD and skinned knees. And we aspired to be them.

- Nick Arcade: This was what happened when early CGI nightmares were turned into a game. Kids answered video game trivia, then got teleported into a green screen hellscape where they flailed around like confused Sims trying to fight a dragon with no weapon. The host was hyped, the audience was confused, and no one—NO ONE—ever beat the final boss. It was like watching digital purgatory, and it was glorious.

- Figure It Out: This was the "Guess Who" of bodily talents. A kid could squirt milk out of their eye or play Beethoven on their toes, and a panel of C-list Nickelodeon celebrities had to guess the talent by asking yes or no questions. You'd sit there thinking, "Wait... someone can do WHAT with a trumpet and a pogo stick?" And it always ended in slime. Always. You could've guessed the answer in two seconds—you were still getting slimed. No one left clean. No one left proud.

- Wild & Crazy Kids: A fever dream of outdoor games that felt like gym class on meth. Giant water balloon fights. Tug-of-war over a pool. Dodgeball with paint. The kind of events where one wrong move could dislocate a shoulder or cause a full-on asthma attack. But damn it, it looked FUN. You didn't want to win. You just wanted to be in it.

Then we had the rest of the 80s and 90s game show galaxy:

- Fun House: Basically Double Dare's chaotic cousin who wore a leather jacket and smoked behind the school. It had all the slime and climbing and confusion but somehow more dangerous. You ran through rooms ripping tags off walls like a looter in a cartoon riot. And the host, J.D. Roth, had the energy of a youth pastor with too much Surge in his system.

- Finders Keepers: A show where kids trashed entire rooms looking for hidden objects like they were on a sugar bender. This is what would happen if you let raccoons loose in an IKEA.

- Make the Grade: A quiz show disguised as an educational game, but we all knew it was just a filler while we waited for more slime.

- Think Fast!: Hosted by someone who always looked like they just rolled out of bed. The games made no sense, the set looked like it was designed by someone on mushrooms, and yet it was perfect.

We weren't just watching these shows. We were training for them. Every backyard obstacle course? Inspired by the Crag. Every living room scavenger hunt? Temple Run in our heads. We flipped over couch cushions like they were swinging platforms. We made trivia games out of cereal boxes. We practiced catching whipped cream pies and perfected our "OH NO!" face just in case we got slimed someday.

These shows made us believe that childhood was a contact sport. That effort, chaos, and a good sense of humor could get you further than straight A's. They taught us that getting messy was a sign of success, not failure. That slipping in a vat of gelatin while holding a giant toothbrush was the dream, not the punchline.

So yeah, you can keep your drama-filled competition shows with judges and tears and edited reactions. We had foam pits, temple guards, whipped cream, and enough green slime to flood a city block. And we came out of it stronger. Hungrier. Stickier.

You didn't live until you shouted "PHYSICAL CHALLENGE!" at your TV and meant it.

SECTION 7: TRUE CRIME & NIGHTMARE FUEL – WHEN TV TURNED THE LIGHTS OFF

Welcome to the darkest corner of the Gen X TV experience. This wasn't slapstick or soft piano music with life lessons baked in. No, this was straight-up anxiety content served hot with a side of cold sweats. It was when the screen stopped trying to comfort us and decided, instead, to *warn us*. And not in a gentle, "maybe don't run with scissors" kind of way. No, this was *shock therapy programming* disguised as primetime.

You didn't ask for it. You didn't want it. But there you were, still in your school clothes, holding a Capri Sun, and suddenly the room went silent because the *Unsolved Mysteries* theme hit like a cold wind through your spine. That shit wasn't music, it was an *omen*. One low synth note and your blood pressure spiked like you were being hunted by the ghost of a Civil War widow.

Let's start there:

- **Unsolved Mysteries** was trauma TV disguised as educational programming. Hosted by Robert Stack, who looked like he died in 1963 and came back to host the most stressful show ever created. This man didn't walk, he *glided* through fog wearing a trench coat made entirely of doom. He stared into the camera like he *knew* your secrets. He narrated disappearances, murders, hauntings, UFO sightings, and time travel conspiracies with the same deadpan tone you use when ordering coffee. And they ALWAYS ended with, "If you have any information..." which translated to: "This murderer could be in your attic right now. Good luck sleeping, Timmy."

And the reenactments? Sweet Jesus. Low-budget lighting. Shaky acting. Fog machine cranked to hell. But somehow, that *made it worse.* You didn't need jump scares. All you needed was some dude slowly walking toward a farmhouse in a denim jacket while a woman screamed behind a screen door, and boom: nightmare fuel for *weeks.* And don't even get me started on the *ghost episodes.* You came in for a missing person story and suddenly you're learning about haunted lighthouses, demonic voices caught on cassette tapes, and a poltergeist who throws cutlery like it's in *Kill Bill.* Why? Because Gen X programming didn't believe in *boundaries.* It believed in *ruining Tuesdays.*

- **Rescue 911**: William Shatner out here narrating real emergencies with the same dramatic inflection he used as Captain Kirk. This show had one job—to convince you that *literally everything* was trying to kill you. You could be eaten by an escalator. Fall into a grain silo. Get launched off a trampoline and impaled on a lawn flamingo. Every episode was like, "Here's a toddler who almost drowned in a mop bucket."

And the reenactments were *always* a little too extra. Like, the actors weren't just pretending, they were *living it.* Screaming, crying, covered in fake blood and flour. One minute, a kid's playing with a garden hose, next minute, *boom,* he's dangling from a power line like Spider-Man without powers. And Shatner would just calmly say, "Little Jimmy was rescued... just in time."

You watched *Rescue 911* and immediately started scanning your house for hidden death traps. "Is that toaster looking at me funny?"

- **America's Most Wanted**: John Walsh didn't do this show for the clout. This was a revenge mission. He had the energy of someone who *dared* you to run. This wasn't just a show—this was neighborhood surveillance with a production budget. Every fugitive looked like someone your mom dated. The composite sketches? Done by a sleep-deprived courtroom sketch artist on a rollercoaster.

They told you about a guy who robbed ten banks, broke out of prison, and may now be working at a Blockbuster in your town. And what did you do? You watched every second, convinced your next door neighbor was the "Midwest Mutilator." And when they *caught* someone? You screamed like your team just won the Super Bowl.

We didn't need sports heroes. We needed updates from *America's Most Wanted*.

Let's get into the Satanic Panic.

- **20/20, Dateline**, and every local news station in the country went full conspiracy mode. Everything was a portal to Hell. Dungeons & Dragons? Satan's board game. Heavy metal? Satan's mixtape. Lisa Frank stickers? Probably a gateway drug to demonic possession. And they always used the same footage: teens in trench coats lighting candles in the woods like it was a Hot Topic promotional shoot. One time, a news report straight-up claimed that a kid got possessed because he listened to *Iron Maiden* backwards while holding a hamster. And we *believed it*. Because Barbara Walters said so.

- Stranger danger specials were basically horror short films. They would air a dramatization where some creepy guy in a van offered a kid a puppy or a free Atari, and then *boom*, fade to black, "She was never seen again." That was it. That was the whole message. No helpful tips. Just raw dread.

Some of us didn't even have cable, so we were relying on **Hard Copy**, **Inside Edition**, and **A Current Affair**, which were like *Unsolved Mysteries* on bath salts. Every story was either about aliens, killer clowns, tabloid crimes, or someone getting surgery to look like a cat. These shows had no chill. They went from "Man Claims to Be Reincarnated Elvis" to "Motel Cannibal Loose in Tulsa" like it was normal.

And local news? Forget about it. *"Is your microwave killing your family? Find out at 11."* *"What's lurking in your child's backpack that could melt their skin? Tune in after Cheers."*

Even *Are You Afraid of the Dark?*, which was *meant* for kids, was like, "Tonight's story is about a haunted camera that curses you with death... enjoy your sleepover!" The clown from "Laughing in the Dark" is still living rent-free in my anxiety center.

And finally... the legacy of it all.

Gen X wasn't raised with coping skills. We were raised with *fear-based preparedness*. We learned that danger could strike *anytime*. That your dad could be replaced by a serial killer. That your microwave might explode. That your babysitter might be a cultist. And that Robert Stack *definitely* knew where you lived.

This wasn't entertainment. This was *stress training*. And we sat there, blanketed in fear and static electricity, eating our dry cereal straight from the box like war-hardened little gremlins.

So yeah, we might be emotionally distant and flinch every time a phone rings after 9 PM. But we're also the generation that can spot a red flag in under 5 seconds and lock every door in the house while carrying a plate of Bagel Bites.

Welcome to the trauma channel.

We *didn't* ask for it.

But damn if we didn't memorize every word.

SECTION 8: NICKELODEON & SNICK – SLIME, SASS, AND GLORIOUS CHAOS

Before Netflix queues, before Disney bought the planet, and before YouTube taught your kid how to change a tire at age 7, there was Nickelodeon. And for Gen X, it wasn't just a channel. It was a damn lifestyle. It was orange. It was loud. It was slightly gross. And it gave us permission to be as weird, messy, and gloriously unpolished as we wanted to be. Nickelodeon was the one place that didn't treat us like little babies—or mini adults. It treated us like kids. Beautifully unhinged, chaotic, emotionally unstable kids. And we loved it for that.

THE GOLDEN ERA OF "DON'T TRY THIS AT HOME"

Let's be real: Nickelodeon invented the slime multiverse. Before Marvel had phases, Nick had *phases of mess.* You got slimed, pied, dunked, gooed, dropped through trapdoors, and nobody ever explained *what the hell slime even was.* And we didn't care. We just *wanted in.* You didn't watch Nickelodeon—you *trained for it.* If there was a gym for chaos, it would've had Gak instead of dumbbells.

- **You Can't Do That On Television**: This was a Canadian sketch comedy cooked in a fever dream. Hosted in what looked like a medieval torture chamber, it gave us the OG slime rules. Say "I don't know"? Slime. Say "water"? You're about to get a Nickelodeon tsunami dropped on your head. The show made zero sense, had weird goth energy, and somehow birthed Alanis Morissette. That's not a show, that's *black magic.*

- **Double Dare / Family Double Dare**: Covered in Section 6, yes—but it belongs here too because this was Nickelodeon's Hunger Games. The flags. The pies. The nose. THE GIANT NOSE. No one ever explained why that nose existed, but we *wanted* in. I would've fought a raccoon to crawl inside that slimy schnoz and yank a flag out of its sinus cavity. And Marc Summers? That man hosted it all while secretly battling OCD. A literal hero.

- **What Would You Do?**: This was a chaos machine. There were pies. There were spinning wheels. There were pies. A human hamster wheel. Did I mention pies? There were more pies than a small-town diner during state fair week. There were no rules. Just yelling and dessert-based violence.

- **Wild & Crazy Kids**: Imagine if gym class, summer camp, and a 7-Eleven parking lot had a baby. Giant outdoor games, water balloon battles, tug-of-war over pools of slime, and obstacle courses so dangerous OSHA probably sent a cease-and-desist. Hosted by kids who looked like they had to pass algebra before each episode.

- **Nick Arcade**: You thought it was going to be about video games, but then they green-screened kids into pixelated hellscapes where they flailed around like malfunctioning Sims. Nobody ever beat the final boss. Nobody even *understood* the final boss. It was like being trapped in a Sega Genesis fever dream.

WELCOME TO SNICK: THE SATURDAY NIGHT HOLY LAND

Then came the ultimate evolution, SNICK. Saturday Night Nickelodeon. The block. The vibe. The ritual. If Saturday mornings were for cereal and cartoons, SNICK was for pizza rolls, dimmed lights, and the emotional rollercoaster of puberty in 30-minute segments.

- **Clarissa Explains It All**: Clarissa was *that girl*. She invented vlogging before vlogging existed. She broke the fourth wall, insulted her brother, invented outfits that would make Lisa Frank blink, and turned side commentary into an artform. She had a pet alligator named Elvis. Her best friend Sam climbed into her window like it was a drive-thru. Clarissa didn't explain anything. She narrated her life like a millennial with no filter, and we ate it up.

- **Are You Afraid of the Dark?**: This show was a weekly dare. Ghost trains. Possessed cameras. Evil clowns. Haunted pool lockers. That cursed Zeebo the Clown still shows up in my dreams with unpaid emotional rent. And these Canadian teens? They tossed that magic powder on the fire and told stories like they were opening trauma files from the Department of Children's Nightmares.

- **The Adventures of Pete & Pete**: It was like someone made a sitcom while sleep-deprived and high on Tang. Two brothers named Pete. A superhero named Artie who screamed at mailboxes. Their mom had a metal plate in her head. Their principal might've been a cult leader. The tone? Existential dread meets indie film festival.

- **Ren & Stimpy**: This show wasn't just unhinged, it was full-on *institutionalized*. Screaming, burping, eye-popping, musical numbers about rubber nipples. Ren had violent breakdowns. Stimpy licked things he shouldn't have. It was gross, chaotic, genius, and probably why some of us have dark humor to this day.

- **All That**: This wasn't a sketch show, it was a cultural reset. Kenan and Kel. Lori Beth Denberg dropping knowledge like a lunchroom preacher. Amanda Bynes carrying pure gremlin energy. Pierre Escargot in a bubble bath saying nonsense in fake French. It was our *SNL* and somehow better. The audience was kids, the jokes were weird, and the vibe was unmatched.

- **Kenan & Kel**: The duo of dreams. Kel loved orange soda. Kenan schemed like a broke Lex Luthor. They had timing, chemistry, and episodes that involved everything from fix-

ing TVs to accidentally buying a car with peanuts. It was so
dumb and so perfect.

LET'S TALK ABOUT THE DEEP CUTS

- **Hey Dude**: A sitcom at a dusty-ass dude ranch. Teens in
cowboy hats. Horse shenanigans. Mild flirting. The lead guy
looked like he was 35 and working off a DUI. It was dusty,
awkward, and pure Gen X comfort TV.

- **Salute Your Shorts**: This was peak camp energy. The
theme song was burned into our souls. Donkeylips. Budnick.
Ug. Z.Z. We learned about loyalty, pranks, and what happens
when you use an outhouse during a thunderstorm. This
show smelled like bug spray and trauma.

- **My Brother and Me**: This show was short-lived but legendary. The first Nickelodeon sitcom with a fully Black cast.
It gave us Goo Punch. It gave us real sibling energy. And it
gave us Dee Dee, a protagonist so awkward you wanted to
hug and slap him at the same time.

- **Roundhouse**: You never knew what the hell was going
on. Dance numbers. Musical sketches. Emotional moments.
It felt like the drama club got locked in a studio overnight
and just started *doing things.*

- **The Secret World of Alex Mack**: A girl gets hit with a
truck full of glowing chemicals and turns into liquid. Nobody
calls 911. She just becomes a teen mutant with telekinesis
and identity issues. Honestly? It ruled.

- **Welcome Freshmen**: This show was sketch comedy mashed with high school awkwardness. Nobody remembers it. But if you do? You're elite.

- **The Mystery Files of Shelby Woo**: A teenage girl solving crimes with her grandpa? Low-budget *Murder, She Wrote* for kids. Loved every second.

NICKELODEON WASN'T A NETWORK. IT WAS A RELIGION.

We lived by the slime. We died by the game show obstacle course. We memorized every jingle. We stayed up for SNICK. We worshipped Stick Stickly and waited for Big Help marathons. We begged for Floam and Gak and splattered orange splat logos on our school binders like war paint.

Nickelodeon didn't coddle us. It handed us a whipped cream pie and said, "Handle it."

It raised the loud, the weird, the misunderstood. It raised the class clowns and the quiet kids. The slime-covered, joke-cracking, cereal-eating chaos demons of Gen X.

And that, my friend, is *peak television history*.

You weren't a Nick kid.

You were *built* by Nickelodeon.

And we never washed the slime off.

SECTION 9: PBS AND THE SMART STUFF THAT STILL SLAPS – EDUCATION, EMOTION, AND UNLICENSED THERAPY

If Nickelodeon was the chaos agent of Gen X childhood, PBS was the soft-spoken elder who showed up with snacks, life lessons, and a sweater vest. It was calm. It was quiet. It was public. It was *FREE.* No cable? No problem. PBS was always there, broadcasting directly into your soul with a mixture of puppets, jazz piano, and inexplicably intense feelings about community and self-worth.

This was the stuff that *educated* us. It was the reason you knew what a tessellation was before you knew how to do your own laundry. It was why you could say "photosynthesis" with your chest while wearing a Ninja Turtles shirt and eating SpaghettiOs straight from the can.

Let's break it down, shall we?

MR. ROGERS' NEIGHBORHOOD – THE SOFT-SPOKEN KING OF EMOTIONAL INTELLIGENCE

Fred Rogers didn't raise his voice. He didn't need to. He *looked through the screen* and into your little latchkey soul and said, "You matter." And you *believed him.*

This man walked in every episode, changed into comfy sneakers and a cardigan like he was settling in for a full-on existential vibe check, and then proceeded to unpack human decency like it was gospel. And it WAS.

He taught us how crayons were made. He taught us how to feed the fish. He taught us that it was okay to feel mad, or sad, or confused, and that feelings don't make you bad, they just *make you hu-*

man. My man addressed *divorce, death, racism, war,* and *self-worth...* before *4 p.m.* on a Tuesday.

And he had puppets! In a make-believe kingdom! Where a cat named Henrietta meowed through full sentences and a paranoid king named Friday XIII ruled with irrational anxiety and a heart of gold.

And you know what? It *worked*. That show was our first therapy session. It was a gentle exorcism of childhood stress disguised as a trolley ride. Mr. Rogers didn't entertain us. He *healed* us.

READING RAINBOW – THE BOOK CLUB THAT MADE YOU FEEL LIKE A SCHOLAR

LeVar Burton could've read the back of a cereal box and we would've cried. *Reading Rainbow* made you believe that books weren't just things, they were *portals*. And every episode was a journey. The music hit, LeVar smiled at you through the screen, and boom, you were flying through a solar system of literature, feelings, and imagination.

The segments weren't just "here's a book," they were "let's visit a jelly bean factory and then talk about grief with a five-year-old." Somehow it all made sense. And the real kids doing book reviews? Gold. One kid had a speech impediment and still went HARD recommending "Where the Sidewalk Ends" and I swear I would've followed that child into war.

And then there was the theme song. Don't even lie—you know it:

◈ "Butterfly in the skyyyyyyy... I can go twice as hiiiiiiiiigh!" ◈

That song was a spiritual awakening. It's burned into Gen X memory like a branding iron dipped in hope.

SESAME STREET – URBAN EDUCATION WITH PUPPET SASS

This wasn't just a kids' show. This was *the block*. Sesame Street was our first exposure to community living, emotional diversity, and the unspoken truth that everyone's a little messed up and that's okay.

We had Oscar the Grouch, who lived in a trash can and was *relatable*. Big Bird was clearly processing something big. Snuffle-upagus was either imaginary or a metaphor for unacknowledged depression. Elmo had toddler chaos energy. Grover was neurotic and lovable. Bert and Ernie were the original odd couple with more tension than half the cast of Friends.

And *the humans*? They were the truth. Maria, Luis, Gordon, Susan—they were stable, kind, and spoke to you like a real person. The episode when Mr. Hooper died? That hit like a ton of bricks in a pillow fort. They didn't gloss it over. They let Big Bird cry. They let *us* cry. It was brutal and beautiful.

Also, let's not act like Sesame Street wasn't weirdly *funny*. The skits? Legendary. The pinball number song? Fire. The "Yip Yip" aliens? Iconic. Cookie Monster's existential breakdowns over baked goods? Award-worthy. And The Count? My guy turned math into a gothic art form.

3-2-1 CONTACT – NERD COOL BEFORE NERD WAS COOL

This was the science show with a soundtrack. Funky intro? Check. Science experiments that looked dangerous? Hell yes. The hosts were multicultural, intelligent, and somehow made learning about static electricity look like club culture.

And then there was *The Bloodhound Gang*—a detective segment buried inside the show like a bonus track. A gang of kids solving crimes using SCIENCE. I didn't know what forensic analysis was, but I knew I wanted to be part of it. They solved mysteries using logic and magnifying glasses and I swear that segment birthed half the CSI fandom before CSI even existed.

SQUARE ONE TV – MATH WITH A SIDE OF LUNACY

This show was what happened when a math teacher took acid and decided to start a variety show.

It had sketches, musical numbers, parody game shows (*Mathman!*) and the GOAT detective noir segment: **Mathnet**. George Frankly and Kate Monday (later Pat Tuesday) solving crimes *with arithmetic.* They took down counterfeiters, kidnappers, and international jewel thieves using *fractions.* I watched those fools triangulate a car's location using algebra and thought I was watching the FBI.

You haven't lived until you've seen a man dramatically whisper "carry the one..." and then arrest someone.

GHOSTWRITER – LITERACY MEETS GHOST POSSESSION

This show was half education, half supernatural thriller. A ghost that only kids could see helped them solve crimes by rearranging letters in the air like a haunted Wordle. There were actual stakes. Episodes had cliffhangers. Characters were kidnapped, framed, and manipulated by *cyber-bullies before cyberbullying was even a thing.*

Also, one villain literally wrote racist graffiti on school lockers and the show straight-up addressed it. PBS was not playing games. Ghostwriter didn't just help you read. He helped you *read between the lines of society's bullshit.*

BILL NYE THE SCIENCE GUY – MAD GENIUS IN A BOWTIE

Let's be honest: this wasn't "just" a science show. Bill Nye was doing experimental sketch comedy *in the name of knowledge.* Explosions, experiments, puns that made your dad groan, and enough energy to power a whole middle school. The man taught you about mitochondria while surfing on a leaf in a green screen storm. Respect.

His show was science meets MTV. It was loud, funny, fast, and smart. You didn't just watch *Bill Nye the Science Guy.* You *absorbed* it like osmosis through your eyeballs.

ZOOM – THE HIPPIE CULT OF WHOLESOME CHAOS

This was Gen X cult behavior in matching rugby shirts. Kids talking about feelings, showing you how to make peanut butter Play-Doh, and speaking in that weird-ass "Ubbi Dubbi" language like it was a coded message to other latchkey weirdos.

Zoom had no adults. No script. Just kids, cardboard crafts, and chaotic neutral energy. And somehow, that was enough. You *wanted* to be on Zoom. You even mailed a letter to "Zoom, Z-double-O-M, Box 350, Boston, Mass, 0-2-1-3-4!"

ARTHUR – LOW-KEY EMOTIONAL DAMAGE DELIVERED BY A CARTOON AARDVARK

Yes, it's technically more of a late Gen X/early Millennial thing, but Arthur deserves a mention. That show tackled *everything*. Bullies. Learning disabilities. Money issues. Losing a pet. Unstable friendships. All that real-life juice—served in a brightly colored, deceptively gentle cartoon.

And DW? She was a gremlin. An icon. A sociopathic younger sibling who held grudges like a 90s Batman villain.

PBS WAS THE REAL MVP

While the rest of TV was throwing glitter at your face, PBS sat you down and said, "Here's how to be a person. Also, here's how to multiply fractions, grieve the loss of a pet, confront prejudice, and grow lima beans in a window box."

It was calm when the world was loud. It was smart without being smug. It was diverse without making a big damn deal about it. And it taught us things we still carry today—how to be kind, curious, resourceful, and a little suspicious of large yellow birds with invisible friends.

PBS didn't just give us content. It gave us character.

SECTION 10: TV INTROS, JINGLES, AND CULTURAL GLUE – THE INFERNO-LEVEL NOSTALGIA TRIGGER

If you want to understand Gen X's emotional stability (or lack thereof), look no further than TV intros and jingles. These were not just songs or catchy one-liners—they were spiritual awakenings. We didn't *watch* intros. We *absorbed* them. They hit like a streetlight coming on outside when you're mid-freeze tag. They were musical foreplay. The emotional siren song that told your body, "It's time to feel something."

This was the era before "Skip Intro" buttons. The intro *was* the best part. The jingle *was* the hook. We had 22 minutes of plot, sure, but that first 60 seconds? That was everything. It set the tone, set the vibe, and told you exactly what moral compass the episode was dragging you toward. If you didn't sing the words, you didn't belong.

THE HOLY HYMNS OF PRIME TIME

Let's start with the Mount Rushmore of emotional manipulation:

- **Cheers**: "Where everybody knows your name." Don't even lie—you cried. If you were ever even slightly depressed in your life, this song felt like a warm beer-scented hug from the bartender who *gets it*.

- **Family Ties**: That piano intro with Meredith Baxter-Birney and Michael Gross painting portraits of their family? I would fight Zeus to protect that theme song. "Sha-la-la-laaaaaaa." That's not a lyric. That's a *feeling*.

- **Growing Pains**: "Show me that smile again." I dare you to listen and not try to harmonize by the third line. It was church. It was pop. It was therapy.

- **The Wonder Years**: Joe Cocker's raspy-ass vocals belting "With a Little Help from My Friends" over home movies of your soul. That wasn't just an intro. That was generational hypnosis.

- **Full House**: That saxophone alone could get you pregnant. "Whatever happened to predictability?" How dare you ask that question. We *don't know*, but we'll sob about it while watching Uncle Jesse raise a toddler in leather pants.

- **The Golden Girls**: That piano bop of "Thank You For Being a Friend" wasn't just a song, it was a *manifesto*. If you didn't belt it out with your whole chest, you were dead inside.

- **Perfect Strangers**: "Standing tall, on the wings of my dreams." I don't even know what that means, but I'd die for it.

- **The Facts of Life**: You take the good, you take the bad, you take the trauma, and there you have this intro that made you feel like you were learning shit you couldn't even name yet.

- **Diff'rent Strokes**: An intro that starts with adoption and immediately segues into a life lesson about society. That opening told you straight up: we're different, we're poor, and we're figuring it out one laugh at a time.

ANIMATED BANGERS THAT LIVED RENT-FREE IN YOUR SKULL

Cartoon intros were *everything*. They hit so hard, they replaced the need for actual theme parks.

- **DuckTales**: Still a 100% certified banger. When that "Woo-oo!" hits? Goosebumps. Full body.

- **Teenage Mutant Ninja Turtles**: That intro *slapped*. The tempo. The roll call. The fact that Raphael was just "cool but rude" and everyone accepted that.

- **Gummi Bears**: This song had NO business being that *good*. Bouncing here and there and *everywhere*? Bitch, that was about depression and resilience.

- **Chip 'n Dale: Rescue Rangers**: Solving crimes. Making gadgets. Launching thirst traps for Gadget like it was 1991 Tinder.

- **Inspector Gadget**: The first three notes could trigger a dopamine surge large enough to realign your spine.

- **Thundercats**: The animation alone in the intro was better than most movie budgets. You could power a small city off the hype generated by that theme.

- **He-Man**: This man did a full intro monologue explaining his powers like a protein shake endorsement, and we ate it up like cosmic cereal.

- **X-Men: The Animated Series**: Those opening strings made you feel like a war was coming. It was pure mutant glory. If you didn't pretend you were Storm yelling "WIND!" while it played, you are lying.

- **Batman: The Animated Series**: Pure noir. No words. Just music, shadows, and Batman punching the American psyche in the face.

COMMERCIAL JINGLES THAT CHANGED OUR BRAIN CHEMISTRY

Jingles weren't ads. They were *mind control*. They embedded themselves like rogue A.I. in our brain stems.

- "My Buddy, My Buddy, wherever I go, he goes" = friendship anthem of the damned.

- "Crossfire! You'll get caught up in the CROSSFIRE!" = We all screamed this like it was the national anthem.

- "Lite-Brite, making things with liiiiight" = The most soothing ASMR before ASMR was a thing.

- "I don't wanna grow up, I'm a Toys 'R' Us kid!" = We cried when that place died. The jingle was our birthright.

- "Skip-It, Skip-It, skipping and a screamin' all day long" = Skip-It injured more ankles than high school football.

- "The best part of waking up is Folgers in your cup" = We knew that line before we knew how to spell caffeine.

- "I feel like chicken tonight, like chicken tonight!" = We still don't know what that sauce was but the dance lives on.

And let's not forget:

- Kool-Aid Man crashing through walls with a demonic "OH YEAH!"

- Gushers commercials where kids' heads exploded into fruit. We said, "Yes please."

- Creepy-ass California Raisins doing Motown covers in claymation. WHY did it go that hard?

The Kool-Aid Man: A Full-Throttle Sergio-Approved Deep Dive into the Most Chaotic Beverage Mascot of All Time

Let's talk about the *actual menace to society* that is the Kool-Aid Man. You wanna know what Gen X trauma looks like in beverage form? It's a six-foot-tall anthropomorphic glass pitcher filled with diabetes and bad decisions, yelling "OH YEAH!" while demolishing property like it's a tax write-off.

This was not your average brand mascot. No. The Kool-Aid Man didn't *walk* into a room. He *obliterated* it. Drywall? Gone. Load-bearing wall? Collapsed. Your parents' trust in the American beverage industry? Vaporized.

We were just sitting there, trying to mind our business—maybe your G.I. Joes were having a moral debate, maybe Barbie was finally living rent-free in her dreamhouse—and BOOM. Kool-Aid

Man Kool-Aid-Man'd his way through your house like the damn Juggernaut on a sugar bender. No warning. No knock. No sense of boundary or financial awareness. Just pure pitcher-shaped chaos.

LET'S ADDRESS THE REAL QUESTIONS:

1. Why was he even there?

No one called him. There was no text, no beeper, no collect call. Kids would say something like "I'm thirsty," and that was it. Summoned. Like Beetlejuice made of glucose. Are we gonna act like that's normal? That's *demonic*. My man had *portal-jumping abilities* and chose drywall over doors.

2. Who paid for the damage?

Because I guarantee you State Farm wasn't writing a claim check for "Sentient Beverage Explosion." You know that dad in the background was about to hit DEFCON 2. Whole living room turned into a pile of rubble, and here's this smiling MF offering a lukewarm pitcher of cherry regret.

3. What even *was* Kool-Aid?

Powder. That's all it was. Mysterious flavor-colored powder you dumped into water and loaded with an *unholy* amount of sugar. Half the time, the packet didn't even tell you what the flavor was—just a vibe. "Red." "Purple." "Green that probably tastes like lime if you squint." Kool-Aid wasn't about fruit. It was about *volume*.

4. Was this dude even safe?

Let's get forensic for a second. He's a walking glass container. Full of liquid. Moving at high speed. Through walls. I don't care how "cool" he seemed—he was a workplace hazard wrapped in a marketing campaign. OSHA would have had a field day.

5. Why was this okay??

Because it was the 80s. A decade where kids got launched into piles of leaves on purpose and marketing teams were legally allowed to create crack for children as long as it came with a jingle. Kool-Aid Man was basically a sugary kaiju designed to sell you cavities.

THE PSYCHOLOGY OF KOOL-AID MAN (BECAUSE WE'RE GOING THERE)

At his core, Kool-Aid Man was the ultimate embodiment of Gen X childhood:

- Unsupervised

- Explosive

- Brightly colored

- Poorly thought out

- And somehow... *fun as hell*

He didn't ask permission, because we didn't either. He wasn't subtle. He was loud, chaotic, and he brought the party whether the party wanted him or not. In a way, we were *all* the Kool-Aid

Man, sugar-high maniacs busting through life without warning, just trying to be seen and handed a goddamn drink.

FINAL VERDICT:

Kool-Aid Man wasn't just a mascot. He was a *movement*. A cultural terrorist with a smile. The original "fuck your boundaries" beverage. He left behind a trail of ruined houses, jittery kids, and absolutely zero apologies.

And we loved him for it.

OH YEAH..

TV BUMPERS, PSA STINGERS, AND EMOTIONAL SHRAPNEL

- **The More You Know**: One shooting star. One synth sting. One truth bomb from a sitcom star that hit like therapy.

- **ABC After School Specials**: The intros to these were like you were being summoned to your own funeral.

- **NBC Bumper "Let's All Be There"**: Emotional blackmail with a glittery peppy tune.

- **CBS Special Presentation Intro**: The spinning graphic. The trumpet fanfare. That was a signal. Something *important* was about to happen. Could be Rudolph. Could be nuclear war. You had 5 seconds to emotionally prepare.

- **Schoolhouse Rock**: These weren't intros. These were *constitutional amendments* set to jazz.

- **PBS logos**: That creepy THX-level "P-P-P-B-S" computer stutter with that floating head graphic? That was our Stranger Things.

TV INTROS WERE THE CULTURAL GLUE

They stitched us together. Didn't matter what school you went to, how broke you were, how weird you felt inside your own skin—if you could belt out the intro to *Reading Rainbow* or *Silver Spoons*, we were *kin*. These weren't just theme songs. They were our hymns, our pledges, our battle cries.

We didn't memorize intros because we had to. We memorized them because they *meant something.* Because they hit harder than algebra. Because they sounded better than anything on the radio. Because they were *ours.*

This was the mixtape of a generation.

Filed in our brains under "never delete."

Skip the intro?

We'd rather die.

INTERMISSION: THE HORMONAL TRUTH

Gen X Was Horny as Hell and Here's Why

Let's stop pretending. We weren't just curious. We weren't just awkward teens with urges. **We were feral.** And not in some innocent, cute "teehee I kissed a boy at summer camp" way. Nah. Gen X was *simmering.* Our hormones were weaponized. We were running on Mountain Dew, rage, and a desperate need to hump something — anything.

Why? Because the universe *designed* us that way.

Start with the music. The entire New Jack Swing era was a barely disguised mating call. **Jodeci had us dry humping the air in public.** Silk dropped "Freak Me" and we suddenly understood what it meant to "lick you up and down" even if we were 12 and still afraid of French kissing. Even the love songs were secretly just foreplay. And don't even get me started on Color Me Badd. What *was* that man doing with his eyebrows and falsetto?

Then you had the straight-up smut on the radio. 2 Live Crew were banned in half the country, so naturally we memorized every lyric and whispered them to each other in the back of the bus like gospel. DJ Quik had a whole ass *catalog* of freaky anthems, and Digital Underground's "Freaks of the Industry" was the damn *Cosmo sex tips* of our generation. "Lay the towel under the door"?? **Bro, we hadn't even kissed anyone yet. But we were TAKING NOTES.**

TV didn't help either. *Baywatch. MTV's The Grind. Silk Stalkings. Red Shoe Diaries.* And if you were up past midnight? You were playing that pixelated scramble game on Cinemax trying to spot a titty through the static like it was a Magic Eye poster.

Meanwhile, **our parents weren't talking about shit.** Sex ed was a VHS tape and a nun with a ruler. We weren't allowed to ask questions, so we filled in the blanks with songs, sitcoms, *and each other's terrible advice.*

Fashion? My God. Crop tops, chokers, the unholy rise of JNCOs so baggy you could smuggle an entire sex swing in them. Lisa Turtle and Kelly Kapowski had us acting up on Saturday mornings, and don't lie — someone you know once risked it all for a girl wearing *a mood ring and a Bonnie Bell Lip Smackers gloss.*

Also? **We were unsupervised.** Like deeply, criminally unsupervised. We were latchkey kids with hormones, HBO, and a Blockbuster card that somehow always included a copy of *Wild Orchid*, *Showgirls*, or *Basic Instinct* "accidentally" rented by dad.

The result? **A generation that walked around with a permanent half-chub and no coping mechanisms.** We were horny, confused, under-parented, and overexposed. And somehow, it made us *wildly creative.* We wrote love notes, we made mixtapes, we rehearsed pickup lines in the mirror like they were Oscar speeches. It wasn't just about sex. It was about trying to *matter* to someone long enough to maybe get felt up during a slow jam.

So yeah. If we seemed obsessed? It's because we were *built* to be.

The 60s had free love. We had Prince, Janet, and The Box music video channel.

They had flowers in their hair. We had condoms in our wallets — just in case.

TOP 5 SONGS THAT MADE US HUMP THE COUCH (DON'T LIE, YOU DID TOO)

1. **"Freak Me" – Silk**

   Let's just get it out of the way. This song *singlehandedly* raised the nation's body temperature. Those opening vocals? Illegal. If you were anywhere near a pillow when that track hit, it wasn't safe.

2. **"I Wanna Sex You Up" – Color Me Badd**

   You didn't even need to be sexually active to sing this like you paid bills and had back problems. That beat hit and suddenly you were a sensual panther in a Starter jacket.

3. **"Do Me!" – Bell Biv DeVoe**

   The exclamation point is doing heavy lifting here. This wasn't a request — it was a demand. And it turned every middle school dance into a dangerously horny slow-motion grind fest.

4. **"Nice & Slow" – Usher**

   Smooth. Wet. Whispery. Everything about this song screamed "bedroom." Or couch. Or floor. Wherever you could imagine it. Let's be honest — this song made more imaginary babies than any sex ed video could've prevented.

5.   **"Freaks of the Industry" – Digital Underground**

This was the blueprint. The field manual. The Kama Sutra scroll. It didn't ask if you were ready — it *assumed* you were already mid-stroke and needed coaching on stamina. That third verse? Auditory pornography.

TOP 5 SONGS THAT GOT YOU PREGNANT JUST LISTENING TO THEM

1.   **"Adore" – Prince**

You were just vibing. Maybe lighting a candle. Next thing you know, your furniture's pregnant. Prince didn't sing this — he *worshipped* you through the speakers. Every note is baby-making incense.

2.   **"Any Time, Any Place" – Janet Jackson**

You could be in church and this song would still make you question your life choices. Whispered vocals? Check. Raindrop background? Check. Janet softly telling you she doesn't care who's watching? *Congratulations on the twins.*

3.   **"Nobody" – Keith Sweat feat. Athena Cage**

This wasn't just a song, it was an *agreement*. A mutual contract to ruin furniture and call in sick tomorrow. If you made it to the end without heavy breathing? You were already dead inside.

4.   **"Come and Talk to Me (Remix)" – Jodeci**

The remix specifically. That intro alone fertilized crops.

Jodeci had us out here making eye contact with strangers and thinking we were in love. By the time K-Ci hit that "ooh yeahhh," it was already over.

5.   **"Love You Down" – Ready for the World**

This song had zero business sounding like that. It made a generation of teens believe they could seduce someone with a sideways glance and a Members Only jacket. It didn't matter if you were "too young" — that beat said otherwise.

HONORABLE MENTIONS: SONGS THAT GOT YOU HOT, BOTHERED, AND PROBABLY GROUNDED

- **"Pony" – Ginuwine**

This wasn't even a song — it was a *thirst trap beat*. The second that beat dropped, you involuntarily started grinding on the nearest cushion like it owed you money. And we *all* did that ridiculous slow-motion pony ride move.

- **"Between the Sheets" – The Isley Brothers**

An OG entry. This was the cheat code. Smooth, buttery, and grown as hell — this song made you feel like you knew what you were doing when you most definitely did not. Half of us were conceived to this track, let's just be honest.

- **"My, My, My" – Johnny Gill**

Red dress. High heels. Soft music. This song had you planning dates in your head like you were about to drop a mortgage payment. You were 14. But you *felt* like Denzel.

- **"Twisted" – Keith Sweat**

Keith had us thinking toxic relationships were just *passion with better lighting*. You didn't know what was happening, but you knew it hurt good.

- **"Meeting in My Bedroom" – Silk**

They didn't even knock. They just *said* it. Like, "Hey, it's going down. Get in here." This was the national anthem of sneaky links before sneaky links were a thing.

- **"Let's Chill" – Guy**

That title is a damn lie. No one was chilling. You threw this on when you wanted to slow dance into some *terrible decisions*. Ain't nothing casual about Aaron Hall whispering in your ear for four minutes straight.

Parental Advisory:

The following playlist may lead to rapid heartbeat, awkward boners in gym class, and thinking you're in love with someone just because they made you a slow jam mixtape. Use responsibly.

~ 6 ~

PLAYGROUND DARWINISM

*P*op Culture Anchors: Battletoads, metal slides in 100-degree heat

Recess wasn't a break. It was a goddamn proving ground. No adult supervision, minimal safety standards, and the faint sound of *Battletoads* rage-quitting echoing in our bones. If you didn't come back from recess limping, bleeding, or plotting revenge—you didn't do it right.

We were the last generation that considered broken bones a badge of honor. Casts weren't sad. They were walking yearbooks. You break your arm? You get famous for 6 weeks. Suddenly, the kid who couldn't spell "Mississippi" was getting signed like he just dropped a platinum album.

The playground was basically *Lord of the Flies* in OshKosh B'gosh. There was a clear social hierarchy, enforced with tetherballs, Red Rover hits that felt like being trucked by Goldberg, and "accidental" pushes off the jungle gym that always ended with someone biting gravel. We learned diplomacy and betrayal over four square. Survival of the fittest? Nah. This was survival of the pettiest.

Survival Stats (Based on 100% real, unscientific, trauma-informed memories):

- **Jungle Gyms:** 33% chance of glory, 67% chance of head injury.

- **Tetherball:** 50% chance of taking a ball to the face, 100% chance of becoming a war criminal if you "roped" on purpose.

- **Dodgeball:** 10% dodge, 90% eat rubber. Especially if Mikey had a grudge and a grown-man throwing arm at age 10.

And those metal slides in summer? Literal child branding devices. You'd hit that thing at full speed only to instantly regret it halfway down when your thighs started sizzling like fajitas at a chain restaurant. But we kept going back. Because pain = fun. And nobody wanted to be the kid who chickened out and took the plastic baby slide.

We didn't have mindfulness, fidget toys, or safe zones. We had monkey bars, grudges, and a well-honed ability to fake cry just long enough to get out of trouble.

Recess wasn't playtime. It was training. For life. For war. For when your little brother tried to switch your *Battletoads* controller mid-fight. And for every adult situation where you had to smile while secretly plotting your opponent's downfall.

Playground Darwinism was real. And somehow, we all survived. Barely.

SECTION 1: PLAYGROUND ROAST BATTLES – YOUR MAMA WAS THE FIRST CASUALTY

Before we ever got body-slammed in dodgeball or sent flying off a jungle gym, we sharpened our knives in the true arena of pain—**playground roast battles.** And make no mistake, these weren't friendly little joke-offs. This was psychological warfare, the kind that could leave permanent emotional damage and somehow still get you invited to someone's birthday party a week later.

We didn't fight with fists. We fought with **words designed to annihilate your soul.** And target number one?

Your mama.

That's right. Your sweet, innocent mom—the woman who packed your lunch and kissed your skinned knees—was the first fucking casualty. And once the wolves smelled blood, it was open season.

"Yo mama so fat, her school picture was taken by a drone."

"Yo mama so old, her breast milk expired in the '70s."

"Yo mama so dumb, she stared at a cup of orange juice for 3 hours because it said 'concentrate.'"

"Yo mama got one leg talkin' 'bout 'It's time to take a stand.'"

And if your mom actually had a disability?

Too fucking bad.

This wasn't a safe space. This was a verbal killzone. If she used a wheelchair, walked with a limp, wore thick-ass glasses, or even had a weird haircut, she was getting roasted like Sunday dinner.

"Yo mama ain't got no teeth and still trying to talk shit."

"Yo mama rolled into the talent show and ran over the mic cable."

There were **no rules**, no lines we wouldn't cross. You could've been crying about your mom's surgery that morning and someone would still hit you with, "Yo mama got a bionic hip and still couldn't outrun that L."

And it didn't stop with moms.

If your shoes were dusty?

"Look at this broke-ass fool wearing his cousin's hand-me-down LA Gears."

If your voice cracked?

"Damn, puberty slapped you in the throat and walked away."

And if you couldn't clap back?

Game over.

You didn't just lose the roast. You lost social credit, friend groups, and possibly the will to live for a solid 48 hours. Some kids went full silence mode after a brutal roast. Others trained like they were preparing for battle. Watching *Comic View*, memorizing lines from *House Party*, and writing insults in a notebook like a baby-faced Don Rickles.

But if you could hang?

If you had one good line that made everyone stop and yell "OHH-HHHHH SHIT," while someone ran across the blacktop like you dropped a diss track? You were a god.

This was how Gen X kids built confidence. Not with affirmations and breathing exercises, but by **verbally slapping the taste out of each other's mouths and laughing about it later**. You didn't need a therapist. You needed one solid comeback.

And somehow, we came out better for it. Thicker skin. Sharper tongues. A sixth sense for detecting bullshit in adulthood because we'd already survived the most savage court on earth—a playground lunch table where the only real rule was **"don't get caught slippin'."**

We weren't bullies.

We were **battle-tested assholes with hearts of gold,** handing out insults like they were snack-sized Snickers.

Friendship wasn't gentle.

It was roasting someone's entire bloodline and still splitting a Capri Sun with them afterward.
Because that's just how we showed love.

Fuck your feelings. Pass the Gushers.

SECTION 2: RED ROVER & DODGEBALL – CHILDHOOD ASSAULT DISGUISED AS TEAM SPORTS

Let's get something straight: **Red Rover and Dodgeball weren't games.** They were government-funded middle school fight clubs. They were soft-launch violence disguised as "group activity," where the object of fun was very clearly to fuck each other up. And it was all done under the watchful, uncaring gaze of a teacher with a whistle and zero interest in saving your ass.

Red Rover, Red Rover, send someone's soul right over.

This game was a war crime in khakis and light-up sneakers. You line up two sides of kids, link arms, and shout a name like you're casting a spell. Then that poor bastard has to sprint toward a human clothesline and try to break through it like the Kool-Aid Man. Only instead of "Ohhh yeah," what usually came out was "UGHHH SHIT" followed by teeth clenching and a slow roll into the dirt.

And here's the kicker. If you were one of the kids holding the line and you let someone break through? That was betrayal. Your own team would turn on you like you sold state secrets.

"Why'd you let him through, bro?"

"You didn't lock arms tight enough."

"You weak as hell."

That's how friendships ended. You'd be sitting together at lunch on Monday, and by Tuesday, you're on opposite teams, calling each other names and praying you get to pick them next round so you can send them.

If you broke through the line? You were a god for 30 seconds. A legend. People looked at you differently in math class. But if you bounced off like a rubber chicken and flopped to the ground? Congratulations, you just became the joke for the next two weeks. Hope your mom packed extra cookies, because you'll need emotional support.

And as bad as that was, it was just the appetizer.

Because then there was **Dodgeball**, the main course in childhood humiliation and soft tissue damage.

First of all, I don't know who decided that arming hormonal preteens with industrial-strength rubber orbs and encouraging them to target each other's faces was a good idea, but that person belongs on a list. This was not gym class. This was Thunderdome, and Coach was only half-paying attention while eating sunflower seeds and nursing a hangover.

The balls were red. Big. Textured. Heavy.

They made a sound when they hit you, like a fucking sonic boom.

THWOMP.

And suddenly you're on the ground, trying to remember your own name.

There were no soft foam balls back then. If you got hit in the stomach, you'd double over like you just got shot. Take one to the face? Instant glasses break, nosebleed, or temporary blindness.

That shit could reset your jaw. But nobody cared. In fact, if you took a shot to the dome and stayed standing, you were now feared.

There was always one psycho on each team. Some kid who was already shaving and looked like he forged his birth certificate. He had a cannon for an arm and something to prove. His name was always something like Cody or AJ, and you knew when he got the ball, somebody's day was about to get ruined. He'd narrow his eyes, wind up like Randy Johnson, and fire that ball with the kind of rage only kids with divorced parents could summon.

And God help you if you were the last person left. That moment was pure existential dread. Five kids lined up across from you like a firing squad, and you're just trying to survive. You start doing Matrix moves, jumping, dodging, spinning, praying someone trips or the bell rings. And when you catch a ball and bring a teammate back in? That's your comeback arc. That's your Rocky moment.

But then there's the betrayal. You catch a ball, you swear it was clean, but someone yells:

"It bounced first."

"You were out already."

"That doesn't count."

Cue the chaos. Suddenly it's the People's Court in the middle of P.E. and everyone's yelling over each other while Coach stares off into the distance like he's hearing a war flashback. No one knows the rules. The rules were made up. Dodgeball was the Wild West with rubber bullets and hurt feelings.

And don't even start with the "girls throw underhand" rule some schools had. Yeah, okay. Until the wrong girl got pissed and whipped that ball so hard it left a welt in the shape of Saturn on your ribs. Underhand or not, pain is pain. Gender had nothing to do with survival.

Dodgeball and Red Rover didn't build character. They built grudges. They built PTSD wrapped in Fruit of the Loom and Velcro shoes. They were playground diplomacy by way of blunt force trauma. They taught us:

- How to duck like your life depended on it

- How to pick friends based on who wouldn't aim for your face

- And how to seek revenge like a goddamn soap opera villain

But weirdly, we loved it. Every single violent, chaotic second of it. Because there was something about surviving that madness and coming out the other side with a new nickname, a gnarly bruise, and a story to tell that made it worth it.

Red Rover was violence. Dodgeball was vengeance. And recess? Recess was therapy... if your therapist wanted to see you suffer.

SECTION 3: THE JUNGLE GYM WAS A DEATH TRAP (AND WE LOVED IT)

If you grew up Gen X, you already know the jungle gym wasn't just some fun little climbing structure. That shit was a full-on hazard zone, a steel-and-splinter monument to broken arms, concussions, and poor decision-making. OSHA wouldn't just shut it down today—they'd burn it to the ground and salt the earth.

These things weren't made of soft plastic or wrapped in foam like today's participation playgrounds. No. We had rusted-out monkey bars, giant-ass bolts sticking out like tetanus invitations, and platforms so high they should've come with parachutes. And they always, always sat on either gravel, concrete, or the worst of the worst: wood chips the size of machetes.

If you fell, you didn't bounce. You didn't get cushioned. You hit, and then you limped. Or you got carried off by two friends who half-dragged you like battlefield medics while laughing their asses off the whole time.

Climbing to the top of the jungle gym felt like summiting Everest. Once you were up there, king of the hill, looking down on your kingdom of chaos, you had two choices:

1. Carefully climb down like a rational human.

2. Leap off like a goddamn superhero and pray your legs didn't fold like a lawn chair.

Spoiler alert: we always chose option 2.

And don't forget the fire poles. Sounds fun, right? Until you realize you're trying to grip a scalding-hot metal pole in 98-degree heat with sweaty hands and zero upper body strength. You either slid down way too fast and annihilated your tailbone, or you gripped too hard and left half your palm behind.

Or the chain ladders that twisted mid-climb and tried to yeet your ass backwards into a head injury. And we kept doing it. Every day. Like idiots. Brave, unbreakable idiots with no self-preservation instincts.

The real beast though? The metal dome climber. That shit looked like a jungle gym built by NASA for space monkey training. And once you got to the top, it wasn't enough to sit. You had to stand, flex, and yell some dumbass shit like "I'm king of the world!" right before someone shook the whole dome and sent you flying like a stuntman in a B-grade action flick.

And don't even get me started on that goddamn slide. You know the one. The metal slide that doubled as a solar panel. By midday it was hotter than Satan's nutsack. You'd climb all the way up, full of joy, only to sit down and immediately feel your skin sizzling like fajitas at a Chili's. But did we stop? Hell no. We lifted our legs, burned our asses, and screamed all the way down like maniacs. Then we did it again.

Every. Single. Day.

You could literally tell who the daredevils were by the number of visible bruises. Kids walking around with busted lips, scabby knees, one shoelace missing, still talking about how they did a "sick backflip off the monkey bars" like that made them a goddamn legend.

Injuries were currency. You show up on Monday with a fresh scrape across your face? Respect. You came in with a cast signed in

five different markers? Fame. You tried to sue the school district?
Lame.

We weren't looking for safety. We were looking for glory. Every
recess was a chance to prove you weren't soft. That you could fall
from six feet in the air, hit your head, cry for five seconds, and still
make it back in time to trade your snack pack for some Dunkaroos.

The jungle gym didn't love us back. It actively tried to kill us.

But that's what made it sacred.

It taught us about risk. It taught us pain. It taught us that being
airborne without a plan is both terrifying and awesome. It taught
us how to be fearless, or at least how to pretend to be so no one
clowned us during lunch.

Because the truth is, no matter how many times we got hurt...

We always climbed back up.

SECTION 4: TETHERBALL TYRANTS – THE SPINNING CIRCLE OF RAGE

If you know, you know. Tetherball was that one so-called "calm"
game that secretly turned kids into petty little tyrants. It looked
simple from a distance. A ball on a rope. Two kids. Smack it, wrap
it. But in reality? It was a high-speed test of reflexes, rage control,
and how okay you were with getting your face damn near ripped
off.

It always started innocent enough. A friendly round, a couple
hits back and forth. But the second someone got cocky or roped

the ball too close, that's when it turned. You'd hear it before you felt it. That deep, meaty *THWACK* of the tetherball going supersonic, flying straight toward your eye socket like it had beef with your entire family.

And when that rope snapped tight and you got caught in the cheek or forehead? Congratulations. You just got branded by a ball attached to a steel cable. You'd walk away seeing stars while the other kid screamed, "IT'S STILL MY SERVE!" like this was Wimbledon.

Every playground had a tetherball god. Some wiry kid with perfect timing and zero empathy. The type who didn't talk much but somehow hit the ball so fast it sounded like a fucking helicopter blade. Once they got control, it was a wrap. You weren't playing anymore. You were stuck defending yourself like a hostage while this maniac grinned and spun that rope like a noose.

And don't get it twisted. Kids got hurt. Split lips, jammed fingers, black eyes. And what did we do? We lined up for the next match like dumbasses ready to prove we were tough enough to take a hit.

There were no age divisions, no mercy rules. You could be a second grader going up against a pissed off fifth grader with abandonment issues and a killer spin. Good luck.

We'd argue over rules, over serves, over rope height. Half the time we made shit up.

"You can't wrap it underhand."

"That's a double tap, bro."

"Nah, that was clean. Do-over."

Teachers didn't even try to ref. They just pretended it wasn't happening, probably too traumatized themselves from getting wrecked by tetherball in the '70s.

There was no trophy. No leaderboard. No prize. Just bragging rights and the satisfaction of knowing you spun the ball so hard someone ducked and ate gravel.

Tetherball wasn't a sport. It was a war dance. A one-on-one ritual of domination, humiliation, and face-targeted revenge. And if you somehow managed to win?

You were a fucking legend.

And look, I gotta confess something. One time I was in the heat of a tetherball match, and shit got real. Like, *real* real. Somehow, some way, my opponent and I just looked at each other and both knew—fuck the ball, we're throwing hands.

It started with trash talk. Then it escalated. Next thing I knew, I had unhooked the goddamn tetherball rope. (I mean, it didn't exactly require a college degree to figure out how to unclip it, but I digress.)

I got that ball off the pole and now it wasn't sports equipment anymore—it was a **weapon.** I swung that bitch like a medieval mace straight into his midsection, and I swear on everything holy, this boy **collapsed like Ricky in Boyz n the Hood.** Full-on slow motion, dramatic fall, gasps from the other kids. He was done. Game over.

I, of course, got detention. But between you and me? Totally worth it.

SECTION 5: BLACKTOP JUSTICE – WHERE THE REAL SHIT WENT DOWN

While the rest of the school thought of the blacktop as the place for organized chaos like kickball and handball, real ones knew it for what it truly was: the courtroom, the boxing ring, and the execution ground all in one. If the classroom was the system, the blacktop was the streets.

This was where beefs were settled. Where someone finally had enough of someone else's shit and said those five sacred words: "After school. On the blacktop." And once those words were spoken, it was on. It didn't matter what started it. A stolen pudding cup. A jacked-up four square call. A rumor that someone said your mom had crusty feet. Justice was swift and violent.

Sometimes fights weren't even about anything real. You'd swing on a dude just because you were both bored and the sun was too damn hot. The blacktop had this energy, this tension. Kids walked around clenching their fists, hyped up on sugar, and just waiting for a reason to throw down. It was like prison yard rules, but with Scooby-Doo backpacks.

There were no refs, no time-outs. This was unsanctioned combat fueled by Capri Sun and suppressed rage. A circle would form like clockwork. Kids would be yelling "WORLDSTAR" before smartphones even existed. And you'd better believe if someone tripped, missed a punch, or cried, that shit would be talked about until 8th grade graduation.

You had the instigators too. These kids didn't want to fight, but damn if they didn't love starting one. "You just gonna let him say that to you?" "He said your mama shops at Kmart, bro." Next thing you know, someone's shirt is getting stretched out and the crowd is already halfway formed. If two kids so much as squared up, the circle would form instantly like magic. It was the most organized thing we did all week.

And don't forget the classic fake-out moments. The ones where two kids acted like they were about to fight, and then just started dancing, or yelling "Psyche!" while the crowd booed. You'd think people got stood up at prom the way kids reacted to a fight that didn't happen. But even then, you walked away with a weird kind of clout. Like you could've fought. You just chose peace... with a little side of mind games.

And then there were the revenge fights. Not the heat-of-the-moment squabbles, but the slow-cooked beefs that marinated over a weekend. You'd show up on Monday already plotting. You'd pick your squad, scope the perimeter, wait for the perfect moment. Sometimes it never happened. Other times? You waited, struck, and everyone knew by the way you dropped your backpack that shit was about to go sideways.

But the blacktop wasn't just violence and drama. It was also the social stock market. You could gain status, lose respect, get cancelled, uncancelled, and rise again like a phoenix with a fruit leather. Relationships started and ended out there. Someone might ask you out during foursquare and dump you before lunch. Rumors spread like wildfire. Lies, truths, half-truths—it all lived and breathed on that sizzling slab of pavement.

It was where you'd first hear someone call another kid a bitch and mean it. Where "yo mama" jokes evolved into something darker, more personal. Where kids found out who they were, and sometimes who they weren't. It was puberty's unofficial testing ground.

And even if you didn't fight, you still had to navigate the politics. Who to stand near. Who not to stand too close to. Who had beef with who. Who just got out of detention and was looking to throw hands on general principle. This wasn't just recess. This was The Wire: Elementary Edition.

Because the blacktop wasn't just where shit went down.

SECTION: HOUSE PARTY DARWINISM (AND OTHER CRIMES WITHOUT EVIDENCE)

Sneaking out of the house to do whatever crazy shit we had in mind wasn't just a one-off — it was practically a contact sport in our neighborhood. Somewhere between latchkey life and full-blown anarchy, we learned that real freedom often came after dark... and sometimes after your parents went out of town.

Sometimes we honestly thought we were learning valuable life skills from movies like *House Party*. And to be fair — we kinda were. That Kid 'n Play masterpiece doesn't get enough credit for how accurate it was. The clothes. The dancing. The chaos. The unspoken rule that every party must somehow include at least one broken window and a neighbor yelling, "I'm calling the cops!"

There was this one party I'll never forget — absolute legendary status. For legal reasons (and to avoid throwing hands with his family at the next reunion), we'll call him "Kevin." Kevin was left home alone and decided to throw a "small get-together." A chill little kickback. Nothing major.

That "small get-together" turned into 100 people.

I'm not exaggerating — it became a full-blown teenage riot. I remember pulling up with a few friends and instantly realizing this was no average party. Half our school was there. The other half of the crowd? Total strangers. Some from other schools. Some who may have just followed the noise like raccoons to a barbecue.

There *was* a fireplace, but the fire? Yeah. That was in the living room — not in the fireplace. Just chilling on the carpet like it paid rent. To this day, I have no clue how that house didn't burn to the ground. Beer on the walls. Holes in the sheetrock. Someone broke a door off the hinges just to "make more room." By the time the cops came, the place looked like a deleted scene from *Project X*.

The damage was so bad... the family moved. *Moved*. Like packed up, sold the house, and vanished. We told people it was because of the market or a new job, but let's be honest — they were running from that crime scene.

But that was just one night. The truth is, we did *so much stupid shit* growing up that it's a miracle any of us made it to adulthood with our teeth, our kneecaps, and our criminal records sealed.

And the real beauty of it all?

There's no fucking video.

No one caught us on an iPhone. No one posted it to Instagram. No one went viral because someone filmed them jumping a bike off the roof into a kiddie pool full of Jell-O.

We did it. We survived it. And it lives only in our memories — or as a blurry Polaroid someone's mom probably threw out during spring cleaning.

We fought with fists, not comments. We made prank calls, not TikToks. We shoplifted candy and dared each other to eat dog biscuits. We rode in the back of pickup trucks. We played with fireworks we definitely weren't supposed to have. And if you told someone you once got a firecracker stuck in your shoe and it blew a hole in your sock — they just believed you. There was no clip to rewind.

We lived in a time when the dumbest decisions we ever made were mercifully undocumented.

And thank God for that.

Because today's kids have receipts. We had rumors. They have surveillance. We had plausible deniability. We could do something monumentally idiotic on a Friday and by Monday it was already an exaggerated legend — "I heard he jumped over a cop car!" "No, I heard he *stole* the cop car!" "I heard he kissed a senior and then threw up on the principal!"

Was any of it true? Maybe. Probably not. But who was gonna prove it?

There was a freedom in the recklessness — not just because we didn't know better, but because no one was watching. We had no followers. No filters. Just vibes. And those vibes usually ended in a twisted ankle, a suspension, and someone yelling "Scatter!" when the cops pulled up.

We weren't content with breaking rules — we wanted to see how far they could bend before they snapped. If someone said "Don't try this at home," we took it as a personal challenge. We weren't adrenaline junkies — we were just bored, unsupervised, and dared each other into temporary insanity.

This was our playground too.

Just with louder music and more felony potential.

It was where legends were made.

~ 7 ~

OUR TOYS COULD KILL YOU

Pop Culture Anchors: Lawn darts (Jarts), Skip-It, Pogo Ball, Stretch Armstrong, Voltron, Thundercats

Let's not sugarcoat it: Gen X had the most unhinged, unsafe, chaotic toy era in modern history. We played with things that could slice us, stab us, burn us, or blow up in our hands. And we *fucking loved* it. Safety standards? That was a concept for other kids. We were test dummies in Toughskins jeans.

There were no helmets. No soft landings. No rounded edges. If it didn't hurt, it wasn't fun. Our toys didn't come with warnings. They *were* the warning. And now that we're older, with aching knees, crooked fingers, and that one weird scar above our eyebrow that no one can explain—we wear those wounds like merit badges.

THE BOY SECTION: PLASTIC CARNAGE, BENT RULES, AND HIGH-IMPACT PLAYTIME

If you were a Gen X boy, your toy box was a war chest. A god-damn arsenal. This wasn't playtime—this was weapons training disguised as Saturday morning fun.

G.I. Joe (with Kung-Fu Grip): These weren't dolls. These were small plastic commandos molded straight from Reagan-era wet dreams. They came with names like Snake Eyes, Roadblock, and Duke, and they were loaded for war. Real war. These guys parachuted out of our second-story windows using stolen pillowcases. They engaged in brutal backyard combat scenarios that would make a Navy SEAL flinch. And if one of their legs snapped off? We didn't cry. We upgraded him. Wounded in action. Given a limp, a tragic backstory, and promoted to General. Some kids had teddy bears. We had psychological trauma and plastic grenades.

He-Man and the Masters of the Universe: He-Man wasn't just a toy—he was a cultural juggernaut on more steroids than a late-80s WWF locker room. He wore fur underwear, had biceps the size of footballs, and carried a sword so aggressive it basically screamed, "I pay child support in blood." The toys were chunky, like they were sculpted out of actual biceps. Skeletor? Dude was fucking terrifying. Like, actual-nightmare-level terrifying with a voice that sounded like your creepy uncle after two packs of Marlboros. Ram Man had one job: headbutt things. And he did it with joy.

Transformers: These weren't just toys. These were advanced geometry problems designed to test your intelligence, patience, and pain threshold. If you managed to transform Optimus Prime without popping a blood vessel, congrats, you now had arthritis by age 9. These things had tiny metal parts that would snap shut on your fingers like mousetraps. And Megatron? That bastard transformed into a straight-up Walther P-38. A *fucking* gun. No orange tip. No neon colors. Just a full-on German pistol you could point at your siblings while yelling, "DECEPTICONS, ATTACK!"

Toy Guns That Looked Exactly Like Real Guns: We had guns that could've starred in action movies. I had a black revolver so real-looking that my neighbor once called her dad to the window, thinking I was about to rob the place. The police didn't think it was cute either. Eventually, kids started getting shot. That's when they threw on those bullshit orange tips and ruined the vibe. But back in the wild days? You could be 8 years old, in cutoffs and a tank top, holding an Uzi in each hand like you were in a John Woo film. We played cops and robbers, except the cops were actual cops now, and the game got way too real.

Hot Wheels & Matchbox Cars: They were tiny. They were fast. And they were lethal. We didn't gently roll them across the kitchen floor. Nah. We launched them off three-story staircases, built death ramps out of encyclopedias, and watched in awe as they flew 15 feet through the air before exploding into a potted plant. And the orange track? Let's be honest. That thing doubled as a disciplinary whip. Your mom ever take off her sandal, *then* grab the Hot Wheels track? That was some double XP parenting. You caught that thing across the thighs and thought, "Yup, I deserve that."

Nerf (Before the Nerf Nanny State): Today's Nerf is cute. It's polite. It's safe. But back in the day? It was like arming yourself with foam-covered vengeance. That first Nerf football could knock the braces off your face if it caught you off-guard. And then came the Nerf Bow & Arrow. That thing could take out a squirrel. Then we got the blasters. Clip-fed, pump-action, semi-automatic foam warfare. Kids were out here posting up behind the couch like they were in a warzone. The Nerf Ballzooka? It was like a mini gun powered by child rage and raw sugar. We didn't fuck around with foam. We weaponized it.

Cap Guns and Bang Snaps: Sulfur-scented destruction. You loaded those paper caps and got that sweet, smoky bang every time you pulled the trigger. If you didn't have a gun? You slammed the caps with a rock like some post-apocalyptic street kid from Mad Max. And bang snaps? You threw those at your friends, your enemies, strangers at the park. One kid threw one at a pigeon. We never saw that pigeon again. We might've committed a felony and just moved on.

Super Soakers: The arms race of the summer. It started with the Super Soaker 50 and escalated faster than any Cold War conflict. You had CPS 1000, 1500, and the legendary CPS 2000, which could literally break a nose at close range. These weren't water guns. They were pressurized water cannons designed by lunatics who wanted kids to be soaked and slightly concussed. You weren't just wet, you were fucking humbled.

Stretch Armstrong: He looked innocent, like a buff beach bro. But inside? Mystery goo. You'd stretch him until he popped, revealing his alien innards, and then tape him up like a hostage. He lived in our junk drawers covered in duct tape and regret. Stretch Armstrong was a metaphor for our entire generation: pushed to the limit, ripped open, held together with tape, and still ready to throw hands.

Pogo Ball & Skip-It: These were balance nightmares wrapped in neon lies. The Pogo Ball was like trying to stand on a rubber landmine. And Skip-It? A spiked plastic ankle tether you swung around until it caught you lacking and launched you into a somersault. We fell hard. We limped. We got back up. Sometimes we cried. Usually we cursed. Then we went right back to it.

Lawn Darts (Jarts): The king of the death toys. Lawn darts were long, metal spears you were supposed to toss *gently* onto the grass. But we were boys. We launched those things into the air with the kind of force normally reserved for Olympic javelin throwers. Every toss was a roll of the dice. You ducked. You screamed. You prayed. It was Darwinism with a backyard grill. We were one bad bounce away from a eulogy.

Thundercats & Voltron: Sharp plastic. Removable weapons. Tiny parts ready to choke a toddler. Lion-O came with the Sword of Omens and zero safety warnings. Voltron? That bastard came in five separate lions that combined into one jagged death robot. I sliced my thumb trying to assemble him and didn't even flinch. I was proud. I bled for Voltron. You think today's kids would survive assembling that thing? Fuck no.

This wasn't just childhood. It was boot camp. It was a training ground for future savages. We weren't coddled. We were *hardened*. The toys didn't come with safety nets. They came with pain, pride, and permanent bruises.

If you made it through childhood without a cast, stitches, or at least a tetanus shot? Congrats. You probably didn't have any goddamn fun.

Everything was cooler if it hurt you.

THE GIRL SECTION: PINK PSYOPS AND SPARKLY MANIPULATION

Now don't get it twisted. The girls didn't get a free pass. Their toys weren't all sunshine, sparkles, and rainbow kisses. No, no—girl toys were laced with psychological warfare, emotional mind games, and capitalist conditioning wrapped in bubblegum-scented packaging.

Barbie: Oh, she looked harmless. But Barbie was a damn warlord. A walking, talking fever dream of unrealistic beauty standards, bedroom accessories, and the kind of emotional damage that takes therapy and tequila to untangle. Her waist? Like a soda can. Her closet? A monument to classism. Her Dreamhouse? A plastic palace where existential dread wore heels. Barbie wasn't just a doll. She was a full-on identity crisis in stilettos.

Girls didn't just play with Barbies. They curated lives. They staged weddings, breakups, affairs, custody battles, murder mysteries, and entire seasons of a soap opera starring blonde women with dead eyes and removable shoes. Barbie and Ken's relationship? More toxic than a Waffle House parking lot at 2 a.m.

My Little Pony: Sweet, innocent, pastel-colored equine fun? Nope. This was cult indoctrination. Each pony had a name like Rainbow Sprinkle Dreamshine and came with hair that tangled the second it touched air. And the grooming kits? Those were Trojan horses for early-stage vanity rituals. Comb. Style. Repeat. Obsess. Cry. Repeat. These ponies didn't just gallop—they carried emotional baggage.

Easy-Bake Oven: Holy shit. Who thought it was a good idea to hand little girls a lightbulb-powered oven and tell them to bake cakes inside it? You ever eat one of those rubbery, undercooked chocolate hockey pucks? It tasted like melted crayon and disappointment. But damn it if the girls didn't take it seriously. Burnt fingers? Didn't care. Uneven cakes? Crying. The trauma from trying to bake a mini cupcake that came out looking like a sad meatball? Permanent.

Lisa Frank: This wasn't a brand. This was a visual acid trip. Neon tigers, dolphins, and unicorns that looked like they were tripping balls on a Hello Kitty rave cruise. The folders. The stickers. The trapper keepers. Every girl's school supplies looked like they were printed by a glitter-obsessed maniac with a soft spot for LSD. And if you *dared* write in her Lisa Frank notebook without permission? Prepare for a full-blown schoolyard felony.

Polly Pocket: Imagine a tiny plastic torture device with doors that pinched your skin, microscopic accessories you could inhale by accident, and characters that were always just slightly too small to hold without going blind. Girls *loved* Polly Pocket, even though half the time she ended up lodged in a couch cushion or swallowed by a toddler. She was cute. She was mobile. And she was a choking hazard disguised as entertainment.

Cabbage Patch Kids: These dolls weren't cute. They were cabbage-headed nightmares with plastic faces and dead eyes that followed you around the room like a horror movie extra. And the adoption certificate? That was their way of guilt-tripping you into forming an emotional bond with something that looked like a cursed turnip. Some kids swore theirs moved at night. I believe them.

Skip-It (Revisited): Yes, boys used it too—but Skip-It was marketed hard to girls. That counter on it? That was psychological warfare. You'd obsess over the number. You'd feel inferior if yours didn't match your best friend's. That thing was the Fitbit of self-esteem annihilation.

Charm Bracelets and Friendship Beads: You wanna talk passive-aggressive warfare? These accessories were a full-blown ranking system of who loved who the most. If your bestie gave someone else a bead that matched *yours*, it was on. Tears were shed. Diaries were written. Alliances were broken. You think politics are dirty? Try playground friendship hierarchies.

The Fashion Plates: This was like playing paper dolls while slowly being brainwashed by the fashion industry. Girls would make outfits by rubbing crayon over plastic templates. It was fun. It was creative. And it was also sneakily conditioning them to value design, style, and having a wardrobe bigger than a human should reasonably need by age 8.

So while the boys were breaking bones and launching themselves into hedges with homemade catapults, the girls were navigating the psychological hellscape of consumer branding and social manipulation. Their toys didn't hurt you physically—but they could make you question your worth, destroy your self-esteem, and emotionally wreck you by recess.

Different battlefield. Same war.

And just like us, they survived. Bruised, broken, glitter-bombed, and gaslit—but tougher than hell.

Playtime was never safe. It was a goddamn crucible.

THE UNISEX SECTION: SHARED ADDICTIONS AND DIGITAL OBSESSIONS

Not everything in the Gen X toy box was divided by gender. Some stuff was too big, too powerful, or too fucking cool to be owned by just the boys or just the girls. These were the toys and gadgets that united us. The great equalizers. The crown jewels of shared chaos.

Nintendo (NES): This wasn't just a console. This was a cultural fucking event. A household altar. A family member. The NES didn't sit on the shelf—it ruled the goddamn living room. Entire weekends revolved around it. Homework suffered. Sleepovers were redefined. Pizza was ordered, sodas were cracked, and we sat cross-legged on shag carpet like disciples waiting for the gospel of pixelated glory.

In our house, Nintendo was king. You didn't *own* it—you *served* it. Mario wasn't a game. He was a quest. Duck Hunt? Target practice for future hitmen. And Zelda? That shit was a spiritual awakening. You were a child with no map and no instructions, lost in a strange land, stabbing bushes and bombing rocks like a tweaked-out treasure hunter. And every secret you uncovered felt like you broke into the goddamn Matrix.

We fought over controllers like it was a holy relic. Siblings were cursed out, smacked with throw pillows, and bribed with candy just for *one more turn.* When the system glitched? You didn't panic. You blew into the cartridge like it owed you money and slammed it back in like a gangster reloading a clip. That wasn't just dust. That was *faith.*

And when that power button didn't work? You pressed it four times, half-pushed the cartridge in, held your breath, offered a silent prayer to Shigeru Miyamoto, and hoped to God the screen didn't flash and freeze. That moment of suspense? That was our version of Russian Roulette.

Mario taught us timing. Mega Man taught us rage. Metroid taught us patience. Contra taught us to never go into battle without the damn Konami Code. If you didn't know Up Up Down Down Left Right Left Right B A Start, you were a peasant. We didn't rent games—we *studied* them. We wrote cheat codes on lined notebook paper. We drew maps by hand. We called the Nintendo Power hotline like little addicts begging for clues.

Nintendo wasn't just for boys. It wasn't just for girls. It was for *us*. It was the great unifier. And when that gray, blocky controller was in your hand, you were the goddamn hero.

Etch A Sketch: You twisted those damn knobs like a safe cracker trying to defuse a bomb, hoping for a straight line and ending up with shaky garbage. Boys and girls alike were united by one thing: our art looked like shit. But every once in a while, someone made a legit drawing and it was like seeing God.

Lite-Brite: Ah yes, glowing plastic pegs stabbed into a black paper grid to form clumsy masterpieces. It was peaceful, colorful, and accidentally painful as hell if you stepped on one barefoot. But it belonged to all of us. Boys made monsters. Girls made rainbows. Everyone made a mess.

Board Games: Operation? Anxiety simulator. Perfection? Explosive stress test. Mouse Trap? Engineering degree required. Battleship? Gender-neutral psychological warfare. Uno? A slow descent into betrayal and shouted curses. These games brought everyone to the table—and then tore families apart.

Pogo Sticks and Moon Shoes: These were equal-opportunity ankle destroyers. Didn't matter who you were. If you owned Moon Shoes, you thought you were gonna bounce like Michael Jordan. You didn't. You sprained something. Pogo Sticks promised fun and delivered shin bruises. Gender be damned—we all limped home.

Slap Bracelets: They were banned in schools for a reason. Everyone wore them. Everyone slapped them. And every single one eventually got bent to hell and turned into a jagged wrist saw. They were fashion. They were weaponry. They were chaos. And we couldn't get enough.

View-Master: You clicked through those reels like you were seeing the world in 3D for the first time. And honestly? You were. Cartoons, nature reels, weird-ass puppet shows—didn't matter. We were hypnotized. It was pure unisex stoner bait before any of us even knew what that meant.

Yo-Yos: You either had the skills to walk the dog or you cracked your own knuckles. There was no in-between. It was simple. Elegant. And it hurt. Everyone had one, no one could actually use it, and we still carried them around like we were nunchuck masters.

These were the shared toys. The peacemakers. The ones that didn't give a shit what you looked like, what color your toy aisle was, or how you identified. They just asked one thing of you:

Bring your chaos.

Because the 80s and 90s didn't play favorites. They just played hard.

THE MECCA: TOYS "R" US

But all roads led to one place. The holy land. The battlefield and the promised land all rolled into one. I'm talking about the one place where a kid could truly be a kid: *Toys "R" Fucking Us.*

Walking into Toys "R" Us was like crossing through the gates of Valhalla. That automatic door whooshed open and hit you with a blast of fluorescent light, air-conditioned heaven, and the faint smell of new plastic and unfiltered joy. It wasn't just a store. It was a kingdom. A temple. A goddamn childhood pilgrimage site.

Rows upon rows of shelves stretching into infinity, stacked high with every toy, game, and gadget you could dream of. Action figures locked in battle-ready poses. Dolls blinking blankly like they were plotting something. Bikes lined up like a neon-colored motorcycle gang. And that sweet, sweet Nintendo display glowing like the Ark of the Covenant.

You didn't walk through Toys "R" Us—you *rushed* it. Like a tiny berserker on a mission. And your parents? They were just hoping to get out without a meltdown, a public scene, or a $200 bill. Didn't matter. The moment you stepped in, it was full-scale war. You grabbed that cart like it was a battering ram and made a beeline for your aisle.

Everyone had a strategy. You hit your section first: boys sprinted toward G.I. Joes and Transformers, girls made a break for Barbie or the glitter-splosion that was Lisa Frank, and everyone and I mean *everyone* eventually circled back to the video game case like it was the Vatican.

The real flex was getting to use the little paper slip system for big-ticket items. Bikes. Power Wheels. Game consoles. You'd pull that paper, march it to the register like Charlie with his golden ticket, and wait for them to bring your treasure out from the mysterious back room where dreams were stored.

And the commercials? Absolute brainwashing. That jingle? Fucking iconic:

"I don't wanna grow up, I'm a Toys 'R' Us kid..."

The moment you heard it, your body entered full possession mode. That shit hit harder than any hymn at church. It was a call to arms. A rallying cry. A declaration of eternal childhood. Geoffrey the Giraffe wasn't just selling toys—he was selling hope. Joy. Plastic-fueled escapism.

But nothing—and I mean *nothing*—drove our imaginations crazier than that goddamn Toys "R" Us Shopping Spree. You remember it. The TV commercials where one kid was chosen—ONE KID—to sprint through the aisles, tossing whatever they wanted into their cart while the clock counted down. That was the holy grail of giveaways. It was the lottery. It was heaven.

Every last one of us thought, prayed, and fully believed that *we* would win that shopping spree. We fantasized about our route. Our aisle strategy. What we'd grab first. How we'd double-fist Game Boys and wrap our arms around Super Soakers. Some of us even practiced with grocery carts at Lucky's or Alpha Beta, getting ready for our moment of glory.

But let's be honest: no one ever fucking won that shit.

Much like the Monopoly game at McDonald's, it was rigged tighter than Fort Knox. The most you ever got was a soggy fry box and a sticker that said you won a free small soda. Meanwhile, the Shopping Spree kid was out there in commercials like a goddamn toy gladiator, living your dream.

Toys "R" Us was where birthdays were scoped, Christmas lists were built, and temper tantrums became legendary. It's where you begged, bargained, and fake-cried your way into getting that one thing you *needed* to survive second grade. It's where friendships were tested and siblings were betrayed in front of the clearance bin.

Geoffrey the Giraffe wasn't just a mascot. He was a spiritual guide. A gang leader. The tall, spotted saint of childhood chaos.

And when Toys "R" Us closed its doors, it wasn't just a business dying. It was the end of an era. An entire generation lost their temple. Their playground. Their battlefield. No click-to-cart bullshit will ever replace the feeling of tearing ass down the aisles with a sugar high and a dream.

We didn't want much. Just our toys. Our freedom. Our chaos.

And damn it, Toys "R" Us gave it to us every single time.

~ 8 ~

WE WERE INTERNET BETA TESTERS

Pop Culture Anchors: AOL trial CDs, Ask Jeeves, Napster, The Net with Sandra Bullock

We didn't grow up with the internet, we *survived* it. Raw. Un-filtered. Slow as molasses and about as stable as a Jenga tower during an earthquake. Gen X didn't just get online, we *forged* the digital frontier while it screamed at us with that iconic dial-up war cry. You know the one. That banshee screech followed by what sounded like R2-D2 having a seizure. It meant one thing: you were connecting to the future. Unless, of course, your mom picked up the damn phone and booted you off.

That noise is burned into our souls. It was both a promise and a threat. A summons to a brave new world that would teach us the difference between a .jpg and a Trojan horse. You'd sit there, star-ing at the "Connecting..." screen like it was a slot machine, praying that this time—*just this time*—you'd get in. And when you finally heard "Welcome," that robotic AOL lady became the sexiest voice on Earth.

Before broadband, before Wi-Fi, before your grandma had an Instagram account, there was AOL. And those bastards flooded every mailbox, magazine, cereal box, and Blockbuster counter with free trial CDs. "1000 Hours Free!" they'd boast, like we weren't just going to use it until the trial ran out and then pop in another one under a fake name. We were the OG hackers, the ones who learned to exploit the system before we could legally drive.

Some of us even *collected* the damn discs. Like trophies. Like Pokémon. Gotta scam 'em all. You'd open a kitchen drawer and find 19 different AOL discs next to expired ketchup packets and that one pair of scissors no one was allowed to use for actual cutting. You'd install one, run out the trial, and then install a new one under a different name. First it was "Sergio S," then "Sergi0S," then "John Connor," then "BabyJesus420." The point is, we kept that shit going like it was a pyramid scheme for dial-up.

We were in chat rooms way before your favorite influencer was born. And *nobody* was who they said they were. You thought you were talking to a 17-year-old named "CrystalBby88"? Nah, fam. That was probably a sweaty 43-year-old named Gary in Wisconsin. But you know what? So were we. No one told the truth. It was all ASL? Lying. Pics? "I don't have a scanner." Translation: I'm a figment of your horny imagination.

There was no Tinder. No swipe left. Just hope, dial-up, and a little blind stupidity. We invented catfishing, and we didn't even know it had a name yet. Every conversation was a gamble, and we liked it that way. It was the digital Wild West, no filters, no receipts, and absolutely no rules.

People had screen names like "SexiLadiez69" and "420BluntKing." You'd make a profile and lie your ass off. You were 6'2", had a six-pack, and owned a Camaro. In reality, you were 5'5", built like a Funko Pop, and shared a bunk bed with your brother. But that was the magic. The internet gave us the freedom to be whoever the hell we wanted. Kings. Queens. Mysterious loners who "loved long walks and Linkin Park."

And let's not pretend like we didn't fall in *deep* with someone we never even saw. We were writing love poems in Comic Sans and sending song lyrics in private messages like we were Shakespeare on caffeine. Sometimes it ended in heartbreak. Sometimes you found out your crush was actually your friend messing with you the whole time. Either way, you leveled up emotionally and probably developed a trust issue or two.

You wanted music? You stole it. Period. Nobody paid for shit. Napster kicked down the gates and let us all run wild through the digital candy store. You'd start a download at 10 PM and pray it was done by sunrise. And every track was a game of Russian roulette, was it *really* "In Da Club," or was it Bill Clinton's voice saying "I did not have sexual relations with that woman" for three minutes straight? There were no guarantees.

Then came LimeWire. The virus king. The public health crisis of computers. One song could bring your whole PC to its knees. Your desktop? Toast. Your family computer? Gone. But we did it anyway. Because getting that bootleg Linkin Park track two weeks early was *worth it*.

My son recently asked me, "Dad, what was LimeWire?"

I didn't even hesitate.

"Son, that's how we used to give our computer AIDS."

It wasn't a joke either. That unreleased 2Pac track with Phil Collins might sound great in theory, but open it and suddenly your hard drive would blow up like it was a car in *The Godfather*. Your mouse would stop working, the screen would go black, and for some reason the printer would start printing 100 pages of wingdings. Your mom would be *pissed.*

And you *knew* better. You *knew* it was fake. But the hope? The *possibility*? That was crack to our digital brains. LimeWire was the original slot machine. It offered chaos, viruses, porn clips mislabeled as "Shrek 3 trailer," and the constant threat of your family's financial ruin—all for the low price of free ninety-nine.

Let's not forget the fake download progress bars either. You'd think the file was 96% done, and suddenly, poof—it failed. That was your night. Ruined. Your dial-up connection would reset and you'd slam your mouse into the desk so hard it squeaked. No therapy, no coping skills—just pure, uncut frustration and raw emotional damage.

Top 5 Most Cursed Files We Downloaded

1. **"2Pac ft. Phil Collins - In the Air Tonight.mp3.exe"** – Promised heaven. Delivered hell.

2. **"Shrek 3 Trailer"** – Spoiler: it was porn. Always porn.

3. **"LinkinParkNewSingleFinal(REAL).zip"** – Contained one 5-second audio loop and 34 viruses.

4. **"DBZ vs Street Fighter.mov"** – Looked like a fanmade crossover. Ended with Goku getting run over by Thomas the Tank Engine.

5.   **"Britney_Nude.scr"** – Not only was it *not* Britney, it broke your taskbar for two months and sent emails to everyone in your address book.

The Rise and Chaos of MySpace

If the early internet was a party, MySpace was the bathroom mirror where you flexed way too hard. We weren't just users, we were HTML gods. We coded our profile pages like they were mixtapes. Autoplay music? Hell yes. Custom backgrounds with sparkles and rainbows? You know it. Some of us dropped black-and-white selfies like we were living in a French indie film. And if your profile didn't autoplay a song the second it loaded, did you even exist?

Picking that one perfect song was like selecting your soul's ringtone. You needed something that slapped emotionally and made your crush stop scrolling. We were out here building emotional traps with Dashboard Confessional lyrics and blinking glitter skulls. We didn't care if it lagged the whole page—we needed you to *feel* something.

And let's talk about the Top 8. That was the original social media beef starter. You dropped someone from your Top 8 and suddenly it was war. Friendships ended. Fists may have flown at the skate park. "Why am I #5?" was the most savage question of 2005. Passive aggression never looked so glittery. And the drama wasn't even private...everyone saw it. You were either in or you were humiliated.

Tom was everyone's first friend, but we ditched him faster than a free trial. Custom layouts were the status symbol of the digital age. And don't lie, you copied someone's layout code, tweaked the colors, and acted like you were the mastermind behind "glow-in-the-dark Hello Kitty goth romance."

The bulletin board was our stage. The "truth is..." posts? Chaos. Those quizzes like "What Flavor Lip Smacker Are You?" told us everything and nothing. And God help you if someone posted a survey and tagged you, because now your whole damn night was dedicated to answering 237 questions about your crush, favorite soda, and whether or not you cried during *The Notebook*.

MySpace was messy. It was moody. It was a hormone-drenched explosion of self-expression and low-key psychological warfare. It was our digital jungle gym, and we climbed the hell out of it.

Chain Emails and the Curse of Little Timmy

You remember these digital horror stories. "Forward this email to 10 people or Little Timmy, the ghost of a dead Victorian child, will appear in your mirror tonight and drag you to hell." And the sick part? We forwarded that shit. Because we weren't taking chances. We didn't *trust* the internet, but we *believed* it.

Some were threats. Some were promises of luck. Some said Bill Gates would give you money if you sent the email to everyone you knew. We never saw a dime, but we damn sure did our part, just in case.

Pop-Up Hell and Toolbar Madness

Pop-ups were digital cockroaches. Close one, five more spawn. You'd end up with 19 tabs screaming at you about free cruises, flashing boobs, and "YOU ARE THE 1,000,000th VISITOR!" Every toolbar installed itself like a squatters' union. Your browser had

Ask, Yahoo, Bing, WeatherBug, BonziBuddy, and probably something in Russian you couldn't uninstall.

We used to have *actual techniques* to close pop-ups. Drag the box halfway off-screen. Click fast as hell. Try to hit the red X without accidentally opening the damn thing. And still, you'd get caught and download something that cursed your computer for life.

The Internet Made Us Mini-Criminals

Every Gen Xer who touched the web committed at least one cybercrime. Whether it was Photoshopping a report card, printing fake concert tickets, or downloading a movie filmed with a potato—we did it. We lied about our age, pirated software, and learned basic coding just to get into porn sites that required "credit card verification."

We weren't bad kids. We were digital rebels. The system wasn't built for us, so we hacked it. One download at a time.

Internet Cafes and Public Library Shame

Before smartphones, you had to go *somewhere* to get online. Internet cafes were grimy temples of teen horniness and homework. You'd check your email next to a dude playing RuneScape while someone else tried to print pictures of naked anime chicks. Librarians developed PTSD from what they saw.

Public libraries became battlegrounds. You'd try to sneak onto Yahoo chat or check your crush's MySpace from a public terminal while your mom sat two chairs over printing tuna casserole recipes. You were a digital ninja. Until the librarian cleared her throat—and the shame hit like a truck.

BonziBuddy and Other Creepy Download Demons

BonziBuddy was Satan in purple monkey form. He claimed to "help you surf the web." What he really did was spy on you, crash your computer, and laugh while doing it. And somehow, *we trusted him.* There were others too—virtual pets, download managers, "free cursor packs" that were just trojan horses in disguise.

Bonzi would pop up and say, "Hey there! Looks like you need help!" Bro, you just made my desktop flash pink and installed 47 toolbars. I don't need help—I need an exorcist.

LAN Parties and Local Network Chaos

Before Xbox Live, we LAN partied. We dragged TVs, consoles, and 100-foot Ethernet cables to someone's garage, hooked it all up, and screamed at each other in the same room. No lag. No muting. Just Mountain Dew, pizza grease, and teenage rage. You weren't a real squad unless one of you punched the router mid-match.

LAN parties were our Woodstock. No sleep. No hygiene. Just raw, unfiltered gaming. If your friend didn't threaten to unplug you mid-Halo match, were you even friends?

YouTube Rabbit Holes and the Birth of the Algorithm

Back when YouTube was still wild and free, you could start watching a "Charlie bit my finger" clip and two hours later be watching a guy deep-fry a Nokia. We watched keyboard cats, laughing babies, and conspiracy theories that made your aunt stop trusting tap water. YouTube wasn't just entertainment. It was an endless spiral.

One click turned into twelve. Suddenly it was 3 AM and you were watching someone whisper to soap bars for "tingles."

We didn't understand algorithms. We just followed chaos. And honestly, it was perfect that way.

The Final Scroll

This wasn't just the internet, it was *our* internet. Messy. Loud. Dangerous. A jungle of stupidity, brilliance, viruses, and freedom. It raised us. It scared us. It made us who we are. We were the lab rats of the digital age, and we *loved* it.

We didn't need filters. We didn't have firewalls. We had hope, hustle, and questionable decision-making skills. Our childhoods were lit by the glow of CRT monitors and powered by pure uncut curiosity.

And if you think we're being dramatic, just know: every single person who survived the dial-up era has the digital version of trench foot, and we wear it with pride.

~ 9 ~

GEN X: THE MOVIE

Pop Culture Anchors: John Hughes, The Breakfast Club, Ferris Bueller's Day Off, Back to the Future, Goonies, E.T., Robocop, The Lost Boys, The Garbage Pail Kids Movie

Let's get one thing straight: we didn't have therapy, we had movies. Our babysitter was a TV set sitting on a carpet that probably had traces of asbestos in it. And that glorious TV, with the help of a VCR that sounded like a fax machine having a stroke, raised us. Fed us. Scarred us. And taught us everything we know about life, love, time travel, and the fact that some dolls want you dead.

There were no safety rails on our media consumption. No content warnings. No algorithm baby-proofing our eyeballs. You rented a movie because the cover looked cool or your friend's older sibling said it had boobs. That was the bar. That was the vetting process. We were handed trauma with a side of popcorn, and we fucking loved it.

THE HUGHES EFFECT: THE SADNESS OF SUBURBIA

John Hughes was basically our teenage grief counselor, and he did it all while chain-smoking in a wood-paneled office full of teen angst. This man wrote movies that made you feel *seen*... and then sucker-punched your emotions with a saxophone solo.

- *The Breakfast Club* put five different trauma cases in one room and made them trauma-bond over lunch and white privilege. It was deep. It was chaotic. And it was the first time we heard that we might be a brain...and an athlete...and a basket case...and a criminal...and a princess. And we all said, "Damn. Maybe I *am* all five."

- *Pretty in Pink* had us believing in thrift store magic and falling for emotionally unavailable rich kids with names like Blaine. (He wasn't a name. He was a *major appliance*.)

- *Sixteen Candles*? Where do we begin? You want racism? It's got it. You want casual date rape? All yours. Forgetting your daughter's birthday? Plot starter. Somehow, it still managed to teach us about loneliness, want, and growing up invisible.

- *Ferris Bueller* made ditching school look like a goddamn masterpiece. Ferris was the hero. But Cameron was all of us—depressed, scared of our dads, and one good push away from destroying a $200k car.

Hughes movies were soft punches to our soft underbellies. They were dreamy and messy and full of pain disguised as teen romance. You have your moody high school shows now, but we had Molly Ringwald crying into a sewing machine.

TIME TRAVEL TRAUMA: BACK TO THE FUTURE

Let's just break this down real slow:

- Marty McFly is a teenager.

- He gets in a car that travels through time.

- He meets his teen mom.

- His teen mom tries to fuck him.

I'll say that again. HIS. MOM. TRIES. TO. BONE. HIM.

And you know what? We just...rolled with it. Because the car was cool. Because the skateboard scene slapped. Because Doc Brown looked like he mainlined Red Bull and lightning.

Back to the Future was our gateway drug to paradoxes, time loops, and plot holes. We didn't care. We were too busy trying to find plutonium or hook up a Walkman to scare the shit out of our parents.

SPIELBERG: THE MASTER OF OUR CHILDHOOD NIGHTMARES

Steven Spielberg didn't just direct movies, he rewired our childhoods. He made wide-eyed wonder feel just as terrifying as it was magical. He cracked open the emotional center of our tiny Gen X brains, poured in some awe, a little fear, a pinch of loneliness, and stirred that shit with a glowing finger.

- *E.T.* wasn't just a story about a boy and his alien. It was a lesson in isolation, in grief, in holding on and letting go. It showed us the kind of ugly-cry love that hurts in your bones. And the image of that little wrinkled alien dying under fluorescent lights still lives in the trauma center of our minds.

- *The Goonies* gave us chaos, maps, yelling, secret tunnels, and kids so feral they'd scare actual pirates. It was a survival manual for misfits. Mouth was a smart-ass role model. Data was a gadget god. Chunk gave us permission to cry *and* dance. And Sloth, deformed, chained up, and heroic—was our first lesson in not judging by appearance. Also, Baby Ruths slapped after that movie.

- *Hook* was Peter Pan with bills, belly fat, and broken dreams. Watching Robin Williams relearn joy while Dustin Hoffman served high camp as Captain Hook hit different, especially when you started feeling like the adult who forgot how to fly.

And Spielberg didn't stop there. *Empire of the Sun, Close Encounters, Jaws, Indiana Jones.* Every one of them aimed straight at your soul and left behind shrapnel.

KILLER DOLLS, VENGEFUL TOYS, AND PARENTAL SCARS

Let's dig in, because this section is where the fear-marinated meat really cooks.

- *Child's Play*: Who the fuck thought giving a serial killer a doll's body was a good idea? Chucky wasn't just terrifying...he was petty, foul-mouthed, and impossible to kill. That little bastard had us side-eyeing every Cabbage Patch Kid and My Buddy doll like they were about to stab us in our sleep.

- *Gremlins*: Cute? Sure. But if you misread the rulebook, and we always did, you were basically unleashing demon Furby chaos onto your house. Microwave murder, stairlift decapitations, and bar brawls? All in a *Christmas* movie.

- *Poltergeist*: This one did permanent damage. A goddamn
  tree tried to eat a child, a clown doll attacked from under the
  bed, and a TV tried to abduct a kid. Meanwhile, the parents?
  Blazed out of their minds in the other room. It was suburban
  horror wrapped in Reagan-era carpet.

- *Pet Sematary*: The moment little Gage came back and
  sliced Judd's Achilles, we all collectively stopped trusting
  toddlers. Also, it taught us that burying things, pets, kids,
  grief, only makes them come back worse.

These movies broke the illusion of childhood innocence. Everything was a potential killer. Toys. Furniture. Pets. And worst of all,
parents who never believed you until it was too late.

ACTION ICONS AND GUNPOWDER DREAMS

Now we enter the testosterone-drenched cathedral of carnage.
Our religion? 80s and 90s action films. Our gods? Arnold
Schwarzenegger, Sylvester Stallone, Bruce Willis... and let's not
forget the splits-wielding, accent-heavy, roundhouse-kickin' mes-
siah himself: Jean-Claude Van Damme.

- *Commando*: One-liners, bullets, and body counts that
  would make a war zone blush. Arnold carried a literal tree,
  fed a man to a pipe, and told another guy he'd kill him
  last—*he lied.*

- *RoboCop*: An R-rated masterpiece that combined brutal violence with corporate satire. Murphy got turned into robo-
  shrapnel and came back ready to shoot criminals, and one

guy's dick, clean off. It was both horrifying and fucking amazing.

- *Die Hard*: Not just the greatest Christmas movie ever. It was about being in the wrong place at the wrong time and deciding to turn terrorists into bloody mist with nothing but a pistol and the world's dirtiest tank top. Yippee-ki-yay, motherfucker.

- *First Blood*: Rambo wasn't just muscle and mayhem. The original movie was about PTSD, small-town bullying, and what happens when you push a broken man too far. Later sequels just said fuck it and turned him into a human WMD.

- *Bloodsport*: Van Damme, in his prime, doing the splits on two chairs like it was foreplay. Kumite chants, underground martial arts tournaments, and slow-motion groin punches. It was sweaty, violent ballet. And we watched it over and over until the tape wore out.

- *Universal Soldier, Kickboxer, Hard Target*. Van Damme never needed more than one facial expression—he just needed legs that could reach your face.

These were the movies that taught us pain was power, vengeance was sacred, and slow motion was always better with synth music blaring.

WHEN CINEMA WENT OFF THE RAILS

Some films weren't just bad. They were what-the-fuck fever dreams on crack. These weren't movies as much as they were endurance tests of the human spirit, cinematic WTFs that you watched with a slack jaw and an internal scream that never quite went away.

- *The Garbage Pail Kids Movie*: This wasn't a film. It was a war crime in VHS format. The costumes looked like melted wax museum rejects, the plot was an acid-trip fever dream, and every frame smelled like expired fruit roll-ups and sadness. It took everything charming about the gross-out trading cards and flushed it into a sewer of irredeemable trash. And yet... we watched. Some of us twice. Maybe even owned it.

- *Mac and Me*: This was E.T. if it was produced by a focus group high on cocaine and Chicken McNuggets. An alien that looked like a dehydrated fetus gets adopted by a wheelchair-bound boy, and the most memorable scene is him rolling off a cliff into a lake. Don't worry—he lives, because product placement saves the day. McDonald's and Coca-Cola are practically characters in the movie. Ronald McDonald himself shows up and dances. This was not satire. This was real. This *aired*.

- *Howard the Duck*: A humanoid duck gets transported to Earth, fights space monsters, and flirts (and potentially fucks) Lea Thompson. This movie showed duck tits in the first five minutes. It was executive produced by George Lucas. No one stopped this. No one asked, "Should we?" They just screamed, "Lights! Camera! Inter-species erotica!"

But it didn't stop there. Oh no. The 80s and early 90s were the cinematic Wild West:

- *Nothing But Trouble* had Dan Aykroyd in a penis nose and Chevy Chase being tortured in a haunted junkyard house. Tupac appears. Yes, really.

- *The Peanut Butter Solution*: A Canadian horror-fantasy where a kid goes bald from fear and regrows his hair using a haunted peanut butter recipe. That hair won't stop growing. He becomes a hostage of an art teacher. Again: this was aimed at children.

- *Rock & Rule*: An animated musical dystopia where rock stars battle demonic forces in a post-apocalyptic hellscape. It featured the voices of Debbie Harry and Iggy Pop. Nobody remembers it, and that's probably for the best.

- *Cool World*: Ralph Bakshi's horny fever dream where animated Holli Would wants to bang Brad Pitt so she can become real. It made *Who Framed Roger Rabbit* look like Sesame Street.

This was the cinematic dumpster fire era. A time when a movie pitch could start with, "Okay, imagine a talking food item with abandonment issues," and end with, "Great, we'll cast Dom DeLuise." Studios greenlit chaos. And we, innocent and hungry for anything on cable, devoured it.

These movies didn't just go off the rails. They melted the rails, snorted them, and then puked them into a Betamax tape. And still—we watched. Because the chaos was comforting. It made our own dysfunctional lives feel, somehow, normal by comparison.

When your home life was a mess, watching a duck in leather boots try to seduce a human woman didn't feel weird. It felt like Tuesday.

GENRE SOUP FOR THE SOUL

There were no rules. No boundaries. Every film felt like someone rolled a dice, snorted some pixie sticks, and shouted, "What if a romantic comedy, but with werewolves?!"

Kids movies were about orphans fighting demons. Comedies casually featured mental breakdowns. And dramas had plots that made you wonder if the screenwriter had ever met a human being before.

Genres didn't exist. Everything was a mashup. And we liked it that way. It was weird. It was raw. It was *real*. Even when it wasn't.

FINAL FRAME

We didn't just watch movies. We *survived* them. We quoted them like scripture. We reenacted scenes on trampolines and with cardboard swords. These movies were our secret language, our escape hatch, and our rough draft for adulthood.

Sometimes we laughed. Sometimes we cried. Sometimes we wondered why the duck had boobs.

But we kept watching.

We kept rewinding.

And we never forgot.

FRIDAY AND SATURDAY NIGHTS AT THE VIDEO STORE

This was our ritual. Our holy pilgrimage. The one thing that could unite divorced parents, siblings at war, and friends fresh out of a Little Caesars booth with two bucks left in their pocket—**the weekend trip to the video store.**

We'd pile into the back seat, usually still sticky from whatever fast food was inhaled moments before, and head toward the glowing beacon of blue and yellow—**Blockbuster**. Or maybe it was **Hollywood Video** with their weirdly upscale vibes and slightly more lenient late fee policies. But if you were really lucky, you had a *mom and pop* spot tucked into the corner of a dying strip mall. You know the type. Bad lighting. Posters in the window so sun-faded they looked like Polaroids from hell. Maybe the place smelled like burnt popcorn and regret. But that *back room*? Blocked off by a curtain or swinging saloon-style doors like some old west whorehouse? We all knew what was behind it. No one talked about it. But we knew.

You walked those aisles like you were making life decisions. Do you go with comedy? Horror? That new release with three empty boxes behind the display because *someone already snagged the last copy* and now you have to settle for Plan B? And you better choose quick, too—because if you stood too long without deciding, your mom would straight up cancel the whole mission and threaten to just go home and watch TV instead.

The new release wall was a lie. Half the time, it was filled with bait-and-switch garbage. But you didn't care. You read the backs of VHS covers like they were ancient scrolls of power. You judged entire films by the absurd cover art and whether the guy on it had a mullet, a gun, or both.

And God help you if you picked something for the *whole family* and forgot to rewind it. That little sticker—*Be Kind, Rewind*—wasn't a suggestion. It was a law.

Sometimes you'd stumble on a dusty gem in the Action or Sci-Fi section that had no business being as awesome as it was. Or maybe you rented something so bad it was brilliant. That was the thrill of it. **No algorithm. No curated picks. Just you, your instincts, and a sea of clamshell cases.**

Renting a movie wasn't just about entertainment. It was identity. It was bonding. It was choosing how you were going to spend your one precious night of freedom before school or work or reality smacked you in the face again.

And the walk back to the car? Glorious. Holding that blue plastic case in your hand felt like you just scored treasure. You'd talk about what candy you wished you grabbed, or how you hoped the tape wasn't too beat up to play. And you prayed the VCR didn't eat it halfway through.

Some of our favorite nights weren't parties, concerts, or sleepovers. They were movie nights, snuggled under a cheap blanket, popcorn in a mixing bowl, and some absolutely unhinged flick on the screen. That was our therapy. Our escape. Our church.

Long live the video store.

But before we close this out, let's talk about the **forbidden zone**—that mysterious back room behind the curtain. Every mom-and-pop video store had one. Sometimes it was just a thick velvet drape, other times it was two beat-up swinging saloon doors that creaked like they were holding back a demon. And what was behind it? Oh, we *knew.* We didn't have to be told. Nobody explained it to us directly, but the energy back there? It was different. It was adult. It was taboo. It was *horny.*

That back room was the adult section. A glowing wall of soft-core sin and skin flicks, each one more ridiculous than the last. The cover art was always absurd—women in armor made of dental floss, men with ponytails and oiled-up abs, titles like *Bikini Car Wash IV, Erotic Confessions,* or *Naughty Neighbors 3: Suburban Booga-loo.* These weren't even real movies. They were cheap, badly dubbed, 90-minute montages of saxophone music, bad lighting, and heavy breathing. And they were *guarded,* by judgment, by shame, and by a 17-year-old clerk who made $4.25 an hour and took their job *way* too seriously.

As kids, we were obsessed with getting a peek. We'd try to sneak by. Pretend we were looking for something near the curtain. One friend always dared another to lift it just a little. Sometimes you got a glimpse. Sometimes you saw a grown man walk out with three tapes and his soul crushed by his own choices. Either way, it was magic. It was mystery. It was a rite of passage.

If you were with your mom and you even *glanced* at that curtain, she'd shoot you a look that could freeze lava. But if you were there with your dad or cool uncle, they might give you a smirk and say, "Not until you're older." And that was code. That meant, "Yeah, I've been in there. And no, you're not ready for the emotional damage those tapes will do."

And they were right. Because if you ever *did* get your hands on one, chances are it was awful. Not sexy. Not exciting. Just weird. Just sad. And maybe that's the most Gen X thing of all, being told there was something forbidden, finding it, and realizing it was

mostly a letdown. But the thrill? The forbidden magic of it? That
stayed with us forever.

~ 10 ~

THE MALL WAS OUR INTERNET

*P*op *Culture Anchors: Spencer's Gifts, Hot Topic, Orange Julius, Clueless, Empire Records, Mallrats*

Where we loitered, flirted, and existed.

Social media was a food court.

Peak consumerism with no credit card.

Before Instagram and TikTok, before filters and face-tuning, before we were flooded with notifications from strangers pretending to care, there was the mall. That was our online. That was where shit happened. We didn't scroll. We **strolled**. Endlessly. Aimlessly. Purposefully pretending to be doing something while secretly hoping to see someone.

This was our digital universe in analog form. Want a status update? Check who's sitting at the fountain. Want to know who's dating who? Follow them on their third lap past Anchor Blue. We weren't tagging friends, we were physically *showing up* and hovering near each other like weird little satellites with braces and starter jackets.

We didn't need a phone. We had eye contact across the atrium.

We didn't need likes. We had real reactions when you showed up
with a fresh fade or a new piercing.
We didn't send messages. We sent vibes from a booth at the food
court, sipping Orange Julius like it was holy nectar.

This was our internet.

MALLRAT ROYALTY AND FOOD COURT KINGDOMS

You knew your status based on where you spent your time. If
you had a mall arcade, that was ground zero for the rebels and the
socially fearless. The goth crew camped out in front of Hot Topic
like they were guarding the last portal to the underworld. Preps
orbited between Abercrombie, American Eagle, and that one store
that always smelled like cucumber melon. And the alt kids? They
lived in PacSun and Anchor Blue, dressed like they were always
five seconds away from a skateboarding montage.

The bus stop kids would linger out front, blasting Bone Thugs
or Smashing Pumpkins from a crusty boombox that doubled as
a weapon. And the shoplifters? Well, they were ghosts. You only
knew they were there after they'd hit their third store and vanished into the parking lot like mall ninjas.

No security guard had enough energy to keep up. They'd just
grumble something into their walkie and keep it pushing, sipping
lukewarm coffee out of a "Mall Cop of the Year" mug from
Spencer's Gifts.

THE FOOD COURT: MALL OF HONOR

Let's get one thing straight — the food court wasn't just a place to eat. It was the beating heart of the mall. The crossroads. The watering hole. The arena. It was where friendships deepened, crushes were scoped out from across Chick-fil-A tables, and teenage chaos simmered under the flicker of fluorescent lights and grease vapors. You didn't need a reservation — just a tray, a five-dollar bill, and the hunger of a thousand latchkey kids.

This was a culinary Hunger Games with sticky trays and squeaky chairs.

Start with the classics: *Sbarro* was your gateway drug to believing mall pizza was somehow Italian cuisine. That triangle of molten cheese and oily crust had no business slapping that hard, but it did. *Hot Dog on a Stick?* That wasn't just food — that was performance art. You knew damn well you were going to stop and watch someone wearing a candy-colored hat slam a piston-sized lemon press into a plastic jug like they were summoning citrus demons. That lemonade was crack, and don't get me started on the corn dogs. Golden-brown perfection on a stick. Crunchy, hot, and somehow more sacred than communion wafers.

Then you had *Orange Julius.* The OG smoothie stand before smoothies became $15 yoga fuel. It wasn't a drink — it was an experience. Part orange, part vanilla, all frothy nostalgia. That waxy cup and the foam ring at the top were enough to make you feel like you had something fancy. Like you were *better* than the kids drinking Hi-C at home. You were living.

And then there were the *elites.* If your mall had a **McDonald's** or **Burger King** in the food court? Game over. You were in a tier above the rest of us. That was status. Royalty. Your mall had fast food royalty on-prem like it was no big deal. You could be dunking nuggets in barbecue sauce while your friends were trying to make do with a rogue cup of Panda Express teriyaki that had half the rice stuck to the side of the container.

Let's talk about *Panda Express* though. That orange chicken wasn't just a meal — it was a lifestyle. And don't act like you didn't abuse the sample system. You'd circle the booth like a buzzard, acting like it was your first time each time. "What's that one? Orange chicken? Cool, can I try it?" Bro, you knew what it was. We all knew. You just didn't want to commit until you had six free toothpick-sized confirmations.

And who remembers *Great Steak & Potato Company*? Or *Surf City Squeeze*? Or *Tokyo Grill* with the teriyaki chicken that came with steamed veggies nobody ate? The food court was a buffet of choices even when you had no money. And if you were really down bad, you'd find someone's leftover tray with some untouched curly fries and pretend the gods had smiled upon you.

Let's not forget *Auntie Anne's Pretzels* — that warm, buttery air would grab your soul from three stores away. That smell could make a broke kid contemplate theft. And *Cinnabon*? Don't even get me started. Cinnabon wasn't a dessert — it was an **event**. That cinnamon-sugar-syrup-slicked center was sticky enough to rip out a baby tooth and tasty enough to make you see God for a second. You knew it was bad for you, but damn if it didn't taste like heaven's armpit in the best way possible.

But it wasn't just about the food. It was *the vibe*. The fake plants. The cheap-ass chairs. The "wet floor" signs that were always out but never followed. It was the sound of soda fountains hissing, trays clattering, and some kid crying because they dropped their last chicken nugget. It was where we met up, broke up, talked shit, ate too fast, and then wandered into Spencer's to pretend we weren't in a food coma.

You weren't just there to eat. You were there to be *seen*. You'd perch with your crew in a corner booth like it was your personal VIP section. You'd lean back with your Slurpee or lemonade like you owned the place, checking out who walked in, who walked out, and who was brave enough to approach your table.

And let's give it up for the underdogs — those weird-ass off-brand spots that served Korean BBQ next to a Greek gyro stand, run by one dude named Sal who somehow cooked everything. They didn't always look clean, but they hit the spot. Rest in peace to every mom-and-pop teriyaki bowl place that never made it to 2004.

The food court was the original third space. Not home. Not school. But somewhere in between — where you could just *exist*, tray in hand, napkin wadded up under your chin, surrounded by your people.

That was community. That was youth.

That was **the food court.**

And it will never be that good again.

ANCHOR STORES & RETAIL ROYALTY

Where you clocked in, cashed out, or just tried not to get fired for hiding in a dressing room

Every mall had its anchor stores — the big names you could see
from the freeway. These were the Titans of Retail, the department
store juggernauts that held the whole damn operation together.
They weren't just stores. They were institutions. Pillars of capitalism. Monuments to sweaters you didn't want and colognes that
came in bottles shaped like Greek statues.

Macy's wasn't a store — it was a labyrinth. Once you walked
in, there was a solid chance you'd never make it out the same way
again. You went in for a new pair of jeans and somehow came out
two hours later smelling like ten different perfumes, with a tote
bag you didn't want, and still no jeans.

JC Penney was your mom's happy place. If Macy's was trying to
be glamorous, JC Penney was like, "Nah, we got socks and school
photos, now go sit on that uncomfortable bench while I use this
coupon." You could get a winter coat, a prom dress, and new cur-
tains in one trip — and maybe walk out with a family portrait if
you got caught up near the photo studio. That sad little corner
with its forced smiles and weird backgrounds? Yeah, that was the
original green screen hell.

Nordstrom though? That was luxury. That was for the kids
whose moms had actual jewelry insurance and drove something
German. Nordstrom was where you went to "browse" because you
knew you couldn't afford shit, but damn if you didn't walk around
like you belonged. And shoutout to the shoe department ladies
who judged your busted-ass Converse with a single glance — you
fueled our glow-ups later in life.

But those weren't the only icons.

Let's talk about the *real ones*. The *core memories.* The stores that made the mall *ours.*

Miller's Outpost.

Now that was a goddamn *vibe*. This was pre-OOTD, pre-fast fashion, pre-"drip." This was *West Coast casual,* denim-heavy, Chola-approved, SoCal-to-NorCal unity. You wanted your jeans low, your shirts tight, and your vibe laid-back but dangerous? You went to Miller's. Before it became Anchor Blue, this place was holy ground. That's where you got your "don't fuck with me" outfit for the school dance or your first pair of pants that made your ass look like you had confidence. And if you got flirted with while standing in line? Instant serotonin.

JW Jeans West.

My first job. My first real paycheck. My first taste of folding clothes while silently screaming inside. This was where denim lived and died. We didn't just sell jeans — we sculpted confidence. You needed Levi's 501s? We had 'em. Wanted Guess jeans with zippers no one used? Got you. Bootcut, tapered, acid-washed, and borderline illegal levels of tightness — we stocked it all. And the folding game had to be crisp. One off-kilter stack and your manager would hit you with the dreaded "can I see you in the back real quick?"

I didn't just work there. I survived there.

Shirtique Pro Shop.

My second job. The place where customization met mall culture. You want your name bedazzled across a shirt? We got you.

You want a *Looney Tunes* character wearing baggy jeans and a bandana? Say less. We made graphic tees before Etsy was even a thought. We heat-pressed everything — cartoon mashups, sports logos, fake Versace patterns, and bootleg-ass Tupac shirts with fonts that looked like they were printed using Windows 95 ClipArt. This was pre-licensed anything. If you saw a Bart Simpson wearing a Raiders jersey, it probably came from Shirtique.

This was sweatshop couture, and we wore it with pride.

Sanrio Store.

Pure chaos wrapped in cuteness. This was where little sisters went in, and little brothers were forced to wait awkwardly outside while "Hello Kitty's Fantasyland" blasted from pastel speakers. But let's be real — some of y'all *loved* it. Keroppi, Badtz-Maru, Pochacco — these weren't just characters. These were lifestyle brands for the emotionally unavailable.

It smelled like bubblegum, stickers, and capitalism. You never needed anything in there, but somehow always left with a tiny pencil or a fuzzy notebook that cost $12.99 for no reason.

EB Games (Before GameStop ate its soul)

This was the epicenter of hype. The smell of shrink-wrapped PS2 games, the wall of strategy guides, the rack of "previously played" titles with questionable cover art — this was heaven. You went there to ask about release dates and stood in line for midnight launches like it was Black Friday in your heart.

And if you ever had to trade in games? That heartbreak hit hard. "Yeah, we can give you $3.75 for *Twisted Metal Black* and *Tony*

Hawk 2." Three. Dollars. And. Seventy. Five. Cents. For your child-hood.

You took it anyway.

Kay-Bee Toys.

The most chaotic toy store ever invented. It felt like Toys "R" Us had a baby with a flea market and then gave that baby five Pixy Stix and a knife. Aisles too small. Packaging ripped. Toys stacked at 45-degree angles threatening death with every wobble. It was **discount toy survival mode**.

You could get bootleg action figures, outdated puzzles, or that weird off-brand remote control car with a name like "Speed Viper X-8000 Turbo Storm" that broke before you left the mall.

Let's not forget the holy trinity of mall music retail: **Sam Goody**, **Musicland**, and if your zip code was truly blessed by the gods of compact discs, **Wherehouse Music**. And for those lucky enough to have one nearby—**Tower Records** also stood tall as the ultimate destination for the music-obsessed. These weren't just music stores—they were sonic temples. Sam Goody had that crisp black-and-white signage that felt serious, like you were walking into a music library curated by a guy in a trench coat who knew every word to every Cure song. Musicland was like its caffeinated cousin, a little more chaotic, but still packed wall-to-wall with cassette singles, jewel cases, and posters you'd later try to rip off the walls.

But **Wherehouse Music**? That was the endgame. Vinyl, CDs, bootlegs, imports, and that rich carpeted smell that screamed "We take music seriously, now go drop $17.99 on an album you could have taped off the radio." They had the good listening stations, too—the ones with headphones so massive they could pick up NASA signals. And Tower? Tower felt like stepping into a full-on cultural archive, complete with staff who judged your music taste in real time and imports you couldn't pronounce but bought anyway to feel cool. You didn't just browse. You **vibed**.

It was where you discovered that one band before they sold out. Where you pretended you totally knew who The Stone Roses were. Where you tried (and failed) to flirt with the cashier wearing a Nine Inch Nails lanyard.

And we loved every second of it.

These stores weren't just places to shop. They were rituals. They were where we clocked in for our first jobs, where we blew our entire allowance on glittery trash, and where we realized some dreams came true and others cost $19.99 plus tax.

They were the pixels of our real-life internet.

And together, they built our server.

HOLIDAYS AT THE MALL: WHERE JOY MET CHAOS

There was no higher chaos level than the mall during the holidays. December didn't just flip the calendar — it flipped the entire vibe. The second Thanksgiving leftovers were in the fridge, the mall transformed into a full-blown glitter-covered war zone. Lights everywhere. Giant wreaths the size of car tires. "Jingle Bell Rock" blasting on a loop so hard it embedded into your subconscious like a virus.

It was magical. It was awful.

It was ours.

If you were working retail? God help you. If you were shopping? Same. You didn't walk into the mall in December — you *braced* for it. Parking lots became battlefields. Grown-ass adults would throw hands over Beanie Babies or whatever the "must-have" item of that year was. Furbys, Tickle Me Elmos, Nintendo 64s, Razor scooters — they all left a trail of tears and layaway payments in their wake.

Inside, the air smelled like pine-scented candles, Cinnabon, and anxiety.

Let's talk **mall Santas**. Some were elite — full beard, twinkle in the eye, looked like they came straight from the North Pole via Saks Fifth Avenue. Others looked like they just rolled out of a bar and threw on the suit in the bathroom of a Sears. Either way, that red velvet throne was sacred ground. You waited in line for an hour just to freeze in panic, forget your list, and smile awkwardly while the disposable camera flash blinded you for a week.

And behind every photo was a mom frantically fluffing your collar and threatening death if you made a dumb face.

There were **holiday kiosks** that popped up overnight like seasonal herpes. Selling everything from engraved keychains to weird flying fairies that broke after one use. You knew they were trash. You bought them anyway. One year I bought a fake gold-plated chain that turned my neck green before New Year's. No regrets.

If your mall had a **Christmas train**, you were living in a rich zip code. A tiny janky ride that ran in sad circles around plastic candy canes while a bored teenager dressed as an elf stared into the void. We rode that thing like it was Disneyland.

There was something about seeing **Macy's all decked out in holiday display mode** that made you feel like you were inside a snow globe. Even if you didn't have money, just walking around with a peppermint hot chocolate and seeing the decorations made you feel like you were part of something. Like maybe Christmas *could* be perfect this year — even if you were just there to make out behind the photo booth or shoplift a Sanrio pencil sharpener.

And don't forget the **after-holiday sales**. January 2nd hit and it was full Hunger Games mode for clearance racks. You were trading in gift cards and unopened cologne sets like you were on Wall Street.

Malls during the holidays were beautiful madness. A shiny, stressful, overly decorated reminder that we were all just broke kids in puffy jackets chasing magic under flickering fluorescent lights.
It was loud. It was tacky. It was chaos.

And we loved every broken bulb of it.

MALL EXPERIENCES: WHERE CHAOS CAME STANDARD

Shopping was only half the story. The *real* magic of the mall was in the *random ass experiences* that showed up uninvited, slapped you in the face with nostalgia, and left you either inspired, confused, or slightly concerned for your safety.

Let's start with the **movie theater**.

The mall theater was where you learned what freedom *tasted* like. No parents. No chaperones. Just a pack of hormone-fueled tweens with tickets to *Mortal Kombat* and pockets full of sneaked-in Skittles. You couldn't hear half the dialogue because someone in the back was quoting the lines out loud, but that didn't matter. You were **out**, and that made it an event.

Double features were a rite of passage. You paid for *Space Jam* and then snuck into *Scream*. You'd leave with your ears ringing, your stomach full of buttery regret, and the vague sense that you just became more adult. Also, shout out to the seats with gum from 1993 still fossilized under the armrest. Real ones know.

And then there was the **arcade**.

The arcade wasn't a place, it was a *state of being*.

Dark. Loud. Flashing lights. Broken joysticks. And the constant hum of adolescent ego and Mountain Dew-fueled adrenaline. *Mortal Kombat. Street Fighter II. Time Crisis. X-Men the Arcade Game. Marvel vs. Capcom* if your mall was cutting-edge. You didn't play for fun. You played for dominance.

Quarters were currency. You put yours on the screen like you were challenging someone to a duel. If you won? Respect. If you lost? Shame so deep it followed you to Algebra the next week.

And if your mall had that massive **hologram ticket redemption booth**? Game over. You'd save up 14,000 tickets just to buy a plastic yo-yo that broke on the ride home, but the point wasn't the prize—it was the *grind*. We were born gamers.

Now, let's talk **mall concerts and live events**. These were never planned—they just *happened*. You'd show up to grab a pretzel and suddenly the local Top 40 radio station was blasting Eiffel 65 while a 98 Degrees tribute band did choreography in front of Bath & Body Works. Half the crowd was confused. The other half was your aunt with her camcorder.

One time they had a **karate demo** at my mall. Full mats, black belts, and one unfortunate kid who got kicked square in the nuts by accident. The scream still echoes through the food court in my memory.

And then there was **WCW Nitro at the damn Mall of America**.

Bro. Legit wrestling. On a Monday night. In the *actual mall.* Lex Luger showing up out of nowhere. A freaking ring in the middle of the atrium. Kids hanging off balconies, chanting with greasy fingers and starter jackets. That wasn't just marketing—that was a *cultural reset*. It blurred the line between TV and real life. For a minute, the mall was the center of the wrestling world. And if you were there? You'll never shut up about it.

Also, let's pour one out for the **Glamour Shots era**.

Every mall had one. And every girl in 1994 has a hauntingly flawless 8x10 somewhere in their family photo album. Feather boas. Leather jackets. Stud earrings the size of golf balls. Hair sprayed into a state of unnatural suspension. That soft-focus filter was working overtime—everyone looked like a catalog model... until the prints came back and you realized your eyeliner had betrayed you.

Even dudes got sucked in sometimes. I, myself, may or may not have been convinced to do a Glamour Shot once, and somewhere out there, there's a photo of me looking like a Mexican heartthrob trying to land a telenovela role, staring into the middle distance like I just dropped a mixtape about heartbreak and karate.

The mall wasn't just a location. It was an experience. A randomizer of chaos. You might find your next crush, your first job, your worst hair decision—or your entire personality—somewhere between Spencer's and Sam Goody. And it never needed Wi-Fi to make history.

~ 11 ~

GEN X: WE CAME, WE SAW, WE GOT PTSD

Pop Culture Anchors: Nirvana Unplugged, Reality Bites, My So-Called Life, the MTV VMAs

There was a moment in time when it felt like the world sighed all at once. Somewhere between the last beat of a New Jack Swing song and the opening guitar riff of Nirvana's *Smells Like Teen Spirit*, everything changed. You could hear it. You could *feel* it. Something cracked wide open inside Gen X, and what spilled out wasn't hope or optimism--it was raw, unfiltered reality. The shift wasn't subtle. It was seismic. We didn't ease into the 90s--we were flung into them, gasping, dazed, and disillusioned. The neon glow of the late 80s faded fast, replaced by a shadow we couldn't shake. That shadow became our aesthetic, our armor, and for many, our identity.

We weren't chasing rainbows anymore. We were drowning in irony and wrapped in flannel.

Flannel, Apathy, and Angst

Grunge wasn't just a genre. It was a warning label. It said, *"This generation has seen too much, too soon. Back the fuck off."* We layered ourselves in oversized plaid like armor against a world we

181

no longer trusted. Ripped jeans weren't just fashion, they were our battle scars. Doc Martens were combat boots for a war no one declared but we were definitely fighting. We weren't fighting the government or our parents or even the system--we were fighting despair, fighting the hollow buzz of expectations we never agreed to.

This wasn't style for style's sake. This was camouflage for the emotionally wounded. We weren't trying to impress you. We were trying to disappear--or at the very least, make you look away.

And the hair? Messy. Greasy. Whatever. The whole idea was *don't try too hard*--because trying too hard was desperate, and desperation was for the weak. If the 80s were about glam and sparkle, the 90s were about dull edges and dark corners.

This was the era when looking emotionally wrecked wasn't just acceptable--it was *cool*. We embraced darkness like it was a warm blanket. If you smiled too much, people thought something was wrong with you. We had seen too much divorce, too much latchkey loneliness, too many fake-ass smiles from parents trying to hold it together. Apathy became armor. Sarcasm was a shield. And if you dared to care too much? You were a liability.

Depression Became Fashion

It's hard to explain to anyone who didn't live through it, but sadness became a cultural vibe. Not performative sadness like some filtered Instagram breakdown. This was real, aching melancholy. It was the soundtrack of our lives, courtesy of Kurt Cobain, Layne Staley, Eddie Vedder, and Chris Cornell--guys who didn't give a damn about your feelings because they were too busy drowning in their own.

Their music wasn't made to cheer you up. It wasn't meant to fix anything. It was there to sit beside you in your darkest hours and say, "Yeah, same."

You weren't edgy unless you had *some* trauma in your eyes. Our heroes were reluctant icons. They hated fame. They hated the machine. They were painfully human in an industry built on image. And that's why we loved them. They weren't trying to sell us a fantasy. They were holding a mirror to our nightmares. And we thanked them for it.

We wore our depression. Literally. Smudged eyeliner. Flannel shirts that hadn't been washed in a week. Band tees like battle flags. Therapy wasn't widely discussed, but everyone knew which bands your soul was bleeding through. Soundgarden, Alice in Chains, Hole. You didn't need to talk it out. You needed a loud stereo, a closed door, and just enough rage to drown out the ache.

Nirvana Unplugged: The Funeral We Didn't Know We Were Attending

When *Nirvana Unplugged in New York* aired in November of 1994, it wasn't just a concert. It was a goddamn eulogy. The set was sparse, the stage dressed in lilies and candles like a memorial service. Kurt looked fragile, like if you stared too long he might disappear. He mumbled between songs. He barely made eye contact. And when he closed the night with *Where Did You Sleep Last Night,* he didn't just *sing*--he confessed.

You could feel the sorrow in his bones. The pain in every breath. His voice cracked like a man who knew he had nothing left to give. That final inhale before the last line? That was the sound of a man about to vanish. Five months later, he was gone.

We didn't cry publicly. We weren't built for that. But something inside every Gen X kid broke that day. We just didn't talk about it. Instead, we played the album on repeat. We memorized his silences. We saw the danger signs too late--or maybe we always saw them and just didn't know what to do.

Unplugged wasn't a performance. It was a goodbye letter.

My So-Called Life and the Art of Silent Screaming

Angela Chase *was* us. She didn't speak like a TV character--she sounded like us when no one else was in the room. Her diary-worthy inner monologues, her awkward silences, the way her thoughts spiraled in ten directions at once--they were our exact brain chemistry on display. And the way she loved Jordan Catalano? It wasn't dreamy. It was painful. Consuming. Familiar. He leaned so good, yeah, but he also disappeared when it mattered. And we knew that ache.

My So-Called Life was revolutionary because it didn't talk down to teenagers. It respected us enough to show the unpolished truth. The insecurity, the betrayal, the way friendships unravel without warning. It spotlighted the queerness, the loneliness, the invisible battles happening just beneath the surface. It showed parents who didn't have the answers. Teachers who weren't always right. It dared to make the background characters the main story.

And Brian Krakow? God help us all, we *were* Brian Krakow. Brilliant and invisible. Longing and terrified. Desperately wanting to be seen but too afraid to be known.

This wasn't *Saved by the Bell.* This was war in a high school hall-way. It was what we were living, minus the laugh track.

The MTV VMAs: Our Super Bowl of Sadness and Chaos

If the VMAs of the late 90s were a person, they'd be our messy best friend--unpredictable, explosive, and always showing up with smudged eyeliner and a flask full of chaos. It was the one night we knew mainstream TV might actually let some truth slip out.

You didn't tune in for the awards. You tuned in for the *moments.* Madonna's makeout manifesto. Nirvana nearly getting banned. Fiona Apple straight-up torching the illusion of perfection. Rage Against the Machine climbing set pieces. Britney shedding her Disney skin in real-time. We watched, jaws dropped, wondering what beautiful disaster would unfold next.

It was the closest thing we had to a shared church service--a raucous communion of weirdos, loners, and loudmouths all agree-ing that music still *meant* something. That we weren't alone. That art could still throw punches.

The VMAs weren't just entertainment. They were litmus tests. For what we still cared about. For what we still believed in. For what we were still willing to defend with our hearts.

When the Music Died (Again, and Again, and Again)

If Nirvana cracked the dam, the murders of Tupac Shakur, The Notorious B.I.G., and Selena straight-up blew it to hell. These weren't celebrities to us. They were sacred. They were avatars of our struggle and our dreams. Losing them felt personal.

Tupac Shakur: The Poet Who Warned Us All

Pac wasn't just a rapper. He was prophecy. His music wasn't about rhyming for the sake of cleverness. It was fire on vinyl. Revolution in a beat. He exposed the cracks in the American dream with the voice of someone who lived in the rubble beneath it. "Keep Ya Head Up" wasn't just a hook--it was scripture. "Brenda's Got a Baby" made us uncomfortable on purpose. Pac didn't want to entertain us. He wanted to *wake us up.*

And then he was gone. Shot down in Vegas like the final act of a play he wrote with his own blood. He warned us it was coming. He *knew.* And we were left with nothing but mixtapes and rage.

The Notorious B.I.G.: The King of Brooklyn, Gone Too Soon

Biggie's flow wasn't just poetry. It was gospel for the grimy. He brought elegance to survival stories. Made pain sound like art. He was a master narrator who told us how it felt to rise up while still being haunted by everything you had to crawl through.

Then he too was gone. Murdered in L.A. Two legends down in six months. It wasn't just loss. It was trauma. The sound of two coasts collapsing into a silent mourning that never really ended.

Selena: The Queen We Didn't Get to Keep

Selena was joy personified. She lit up the stage with the kind of radiance that made you believe maybe--just maybe--the world wasn't so broken. She wasn't just a star. She was *ours.* And her crossover wasn't just for fame. It was for representation. For every

Brown kid who needed to see themselves reflected in glitter and grace.

And then she was murdered by someone who claimed to love her. Her death wasn't just tragic. It was betrayal. And it echoed especially hard in homes that had never seen someone like her rise so high. She was hope. And her loss? It left a silence that pop music has never truly filled.

What We Were Left With

When all the noise faded--the gunshots, the headlines, the candlelight vigils--we looked around and realized that everything had changed. The music industry pivoted toward glossy pop. Labels stopped taking risks. Authenticity got scrubbed clean and packaged for mass appeal.

TRL became our new babysitter, with its countdowns of polished, photo-ready stars who couldn't hold a candle to the rawness we'd just buried. But we still tuned in. We weren't angry--we were exhausted. We had lost too much too fast.

We coped the only way we knew how: with sarcasm, with eyeliner, with long drives playing songs that reminded us who we used to be. We put our grief on cassette tapes. We burned it into CD-Rs. We uploaded it into Winamp playlists and buried it in lyrics.

We didn't heal. We adapted.

The End of Something We Didn't Know Was Ending

The 90s started with Nirvana telling us we weren't alone in our sadness. They ended with our idols being murdered before our eyes.

Pac. Biggie. Selena. Kurt. All gone within a few years. All young. All brilliant. All speaking to something *real* inside us.

After that, we didn't trust joy the same way. We didn't believe in longevity. We stopped pretending things would be okay.

We danced anyway. We laughed anyway. But something had shifted.

It wasn't just the fall of innocence.

It was the funeral of it.

And Gen X? We didn't heal. We just got real good at walking with a limp.

We didn't know it at the time, but all that loss, all that pain-- that was the beginning of us finally growing up. Not just because of the funerals and the music fading out, but because we were also watching the characters we grew up with start to grow up too. When Zack, Kelly, Slater, and the rest of the *Saved by the Bell* crew walked across that graduation stage, it felt like a piece of our childhood walked off with them. When the kids of *90210* swapped their high school lockers for college dorms and adult-level drama, we realized the training wheels were off--for them and for us.

Those shows had been our comfort food. Our background noise. Our blueprint for youth. And now they were dealing with addiction, assault, betrayal, and the collapse of fairy tale romances--

just like the rest of us. It was fiction mirroring reality, and the lines blurred fast. The innocence of the Bayside days faded into the harsh light of adulthood. And we couldn't help but feel it deep in our bones. The era of Saturday morning cartoons was being replaced by prime-time therapy sessions.

We weren't just watching characters grow up. We were watching ourselves.

We didn't get closure--we got wisdom. And maybe that was enough. Not in the sitcom way, not in the Hallmark kind of way. In the real, bruised-knuckle, tight-lipped, keep-moving-forward kind of way. We didn't get closure--we got wisdom. And maybe that was enough.

~ 12 ~

BURNT POP-TARTS AND OTHER
LIFE LESSONS

Pop Culture Anchors: Full House, Saved by the Bell, The Wonder Years, Life cereal

We were weirdly independent but emotionally stunted.

When I look at life now as a parent, I'm constantly reminded of the lessons I've learned along the way. Like the time my son recently asked me, "Dad, what scares you?" Without hesitation, I said, "Clowns."

Yes, ladies and gentlemen — I am fucking *terrified* of clowns. Basically, Ronald McDonald, Bozo (to a degree), and Krusty are the only clowns I'll fuck with. That's it. Everyone else can rot in a sewer.

Naturally, my son wanted to know *why* clowns, so I did what any emotionally damaged Gen Xer would do: I trauma-dumped like he was a tiny pre-teen therapist. I told him how, back when I was around his age and impressionable as hell, my uncles thought it would be *hilarious* to have me watch Stephen King's *IT* mini-series. You know, the one with Tim Curry, who already looked like he hid bodies in a crawlspace even when he wasn't in makeup. That alone was nightmare fuel. But the real horror? After I finally fell asleep, one of my uncles put on a clown mask and woke me up violently. Like *Jason Voorhees jumping out the lake* violently.

So yeah, that's why I don't fuck with clowns. And also why I'm the parent I am today. I don't let my kid watch things before he's ready — because I *wasn't* ready, and no one gave a shit. No supervision, no adult guidance, just vibes and trauma.

The first time I saw boobs? *Purple Rain.* Shout out to Apollonia. I was seven. Let that sink in. Seven. Logic didn't live in our house. Common sense was on vacation. And because of that, I now overthink every movie, show, or YouTube clip my kid watches like I'm a goddamn studio censor.

But here's the thing — I wouldn't change my upbringing much. Because who I am today is the sum of everything I survived and everyone (or *everything*) that raised me: TV and movies. Pop culture. Uncle Phil. Homer Simpson. That weird after-school special where the kid smoked weed once and immediately died. It all shaped me. And now I get to pass it down — a little safer, a little smarter, and way more sarcastic.

Truth is we could survive an entire Saturday alone with nothing but Pop-Tarts, a half-filled Capri Sun, and whatever was on basic cable. And we did it without a phone, GPS, or even knowing our parents' exact whereabouts. We were given keys around our necks and expected to just figure it the fuck out. And somehow, we did.

We were the last generation raised on sitcom morals, Life cereal, and complete emotional neglect. Our parents weren't evil. They just didn't know better-and most were too busy working or surviving their own childhood trauma to notice ours. We learned empathy from Mr. Feeny, life lessons from Uncle Phil, and sarcasm from literally every adult on *Married... with Children.*

Some of us were raised by the TV, the radio, and our older siblings' questionable choices. And yet... those same things are what gave us our fire. Our edge. Our grit. Gen X wasn't just a generation-it was a full-blown survival experiment with sarcasm as our only known defense mechanism.

Our therapy wasn't in a session, it was in the back of a Trapper Keeper. It was the mixtape someone made us, the lyrics we copied onto our jeans, and the rage we dumped into a spiral notebook labeled "PRIVATE" but always secretly hoped someone would read. We learned how to self-soothe using a Walkman, a blunt, and a full-on blackout of emotional vulnerability.

We absorbed our morals from fictional characters and PSA jingles. We thought the world worked the way *The Wonder Years* told us it would-but it didn't. We thought love would be like Zack and Kelly, or Kevin and Winnie, or maybe even Sam and Diane if we were getting dark about it. It wasn't. But we kept showing up anyway.

And still-we showed up.

We showed up for our siblings. We showed up for our friends. We cracked jokes at funerals and taught ourselves how to balance student loan debt with payday beers. We became parents, teachers, caregivers, bosses, and therapists *for each other.*

That's the thing people never got about Gen X-we weren't lazy. We were just *tired* of everyone's bullshit. We were the generation caught between analog and digital, innocence and chaos, hair bands and grunge, Reaganomics and Nirvana. We had to become our own translators, our own defenders, our own damn village.

We saw the launch of MTV and the fall of the Berlin Wall. We watched the Challenger explode in real-time and learned early that even dreams could crash and burn. We were told to dream big by a society that kept underfunding our schools and canceling our cartoons. We saw politicians lie to our faces and adults lie to themselves.

We were told to "just say no" by the same people whose drinks were never empty. Our idea of conflict resolution was watching *The A-Team* and deciding which friend was more of a Murdock than a B.A. Baracus.

We kept our secrets locked in diaries with cheap plastic locks and trusted the sacred power of a folded note passed during 3rd period. We knew that if someone made you a mixtape, that was love. That was trust. That was everything. And if they taped over it? That was war.

And now?

Now we're grown. And weird. And sometimes sad. But also some of the funniest, strongest, most real-ass people walking this planet.

We've raised kids who know how to talk about their feelings because we *couldn't*. We've made homes out of broken families. We've kept every dumb inside joke alive in a group chat with our high school best friends. We still go hard when a good 90s beat drops. And some of us are just now learning how to finally let our guard down and say, "Yeah... I'm not okay."

We're the ones explaining to our kids why our favorite cereal has a warning label now, why our cartoons were so violent, and why we panic every time someone says, "Let's unpack this." We'll cry when a rerun of *The Wonder Years* catches us off guard, but still won't talk about that time our dad forgot our birthday.

We're healing, slowly. Clumsily. Loudly. Quietly. We're buying vinyl again, learning to breathe, and sometimes even telling the truth about our feelings. We know now that we deserved better-but we also know we can give better.

We remember when plans had to be made *before* you left the house. We remember calling collect. We remember having to memorize phone numbers and the anxiety of calling someone's house just to hope their dad didn't answer. We remember that being bored wasn't a crisis-it was a crucible. You found your imagination in boredom. That's where your real self was hiding.

We got our scars the hard way. Physically. Emotionally. Sometimes both. We learned to fight back. To shut down. To grow up too fast. We learned that crying wasn't always safe and sometimes silence was power. But we also learned how to laugh when everything was falling apart.

Closure doesn't come wrapped in a hug or tied up with a bow. Not for Gen X. Closure comes in the form of *understanding*. Understanding that we weren't crazy. We weren't defective. We were just... born into the weirdest, wildest, most unforgiving social experiment ever, and somehow? We fucking nailed it.

We made it.

And to the Gen Xers reading this-whether you're in your 40s, 50s, or still bumping that one CD you got from Columbia House back in the day-I see you. I *am* you. And this book was for you.

For the latchkey kids. For the mixtape makers. For the burned-out gifted kids. For the girls who never forgave their Aqua Net phase. For the boys who wanted to cry but didn't know how. For everyone who ever felt like the world forgot about us.

We didn't forget each other.

And to the generations coming up behind us, trying to figure out why your Gen X parent is both wildly hilarious and emotionally confusing:

We were raised with no manuals, just vibes. And those vibes were dark, loud, and usually had glitter on them.

But we did our best.

And I swear to you-we're still trying.

Long live the weirdos who made it out.

Long live Gen X.

Long live burnt Pop-Tarts and every lesson we learned from the crumbs.

If you're holding this book, it means one of us finally stopped to tell the story. And if you've made it this far, let this be your permission slip to forgive yourself. For the mess. For the numbness. For the defense mechanisms and the awkward silences and the decades of "I'm fine."

You weren't supposed to be perfect. You were supposed to survive. And you fucking did.

We were never the golden children, never the chosen ones. But we were the ones who stood up, flipped off the camera, and said, "Watch me."

So turn the page, Gen X. The rest is still unwritten.

And if you ever feel like the world forgot about you-just know: I didn't.

We didn't.

We weren't built to be icons. We were built to be legends.

Mic drop.

ACKNOWLEDGEMENTS

(Because Apparently That's a Thing)

Look, I wasn't gonna do this. I already spent 200+ pages spilling guts, lighting pop culture on fire, and roasting my own childhood like a marshmallow at a Scout camp with no adults. But I guess this is the part where I say thank you. So fine. Let's do it my way.

First off — to me.

Yeah. Me.

I wrote this beast. I survived the trauma, the Pop Rocks, the Saturday morning cartoons that quietly taught us about death, divorce, and how not to talk to strangers in windowless vans. I clawed my way through latchkey loneliness and came out swinging with jokes, scars, and a memory sharp enough to cut glass. This book doesn't exist without me — and frankly, neither does most of my personality.

To Patsy and Lindsay — the sisters who turned chaos into comfort, and fights into folklore. You two were there for every dumb choice, every sugar high, every low-budget family moment we now laugh about like it was a sitcom. I love you more than my Lisa Frank sticker collection. And that's real.

To the 80s and 90s — what the hell was wrong with you? Thank you for the trauma, the toys, the music, the mad science cereal experiments, and the absolute lawlessness of it all. We were raised on vibes, and those vibes were *unregulated*.

To trauma, sarcasm, and questionable parenting — the holy trinity that made this book possible.

To burnt Pop-Tarts, Kool-Aid Man's destruction of private property, Crystal Pepsi (the GOAT), and every sugar bomb we were legally allowed to consume before 9 AM — you are the DNA of these pages.

To Rachel — thank you for being the one who finally made things right after that cursed Christmas in '84. I see you. I appreciate you. That's all you get, promise.

To Jesse — you made it to adulthood with only partial trauma, which honestly puts you ahead of the curve. Proud of you, kid. You're proof I didn't screw *everything* up.

To Jax — my work in progress, my chaos goblin, my heart. You keep me laughing, questioning my decisions, and learning how to be better. Hang in there, kid. You're gonna be just fine... eventually.

And to anyone else wondering if this book is for them — it is. If you ever rode your bike without a helmet, used a pencil to rewind a cassette, or had to survive a week on nothing but toaster waffles and TV static... this one's for you.

Now close the book and go live your life. Or go toast something and call it breakfast. I'm not your dad.

Except for Jesse and Jax. I *am* your dad. Sorry about all this.

Sergio Serna is a writer, creator, cultural time traveler, and unapologetic Gen Xer who tells stories the way they were meant to be told—loud, honest, sometimes hilarious, always with heart. He's the mind behind the critically underrated but culturally essential *One Nation: Raider Nation*, a raw and unfiltered love letter to the fans who bleed silver and black. More than just a book about football, it's a living, breathing tribute to a movement, a mindset, and a family bonded by grit and loyalty.

Sergio followed that up with the vibrant and inspirational children's book *¡Viva los Sueños!*, a celebration of Latino trailblazers written for the next generation of dreamers. The book highlights heroes like Sylvia Mendez, José M. Hernández, Tom Flores, Ellen Ochoa, George Lopez, Laurie Hernández, Elena Medo, Guillermo González Camarena, and Lin-Manuel Miranda. A second volume, *¡Viva los Sueños! Vol. 2*, is set to drop in 2025, expanding the dream with even more powerful Latino voices, including Sonia Sotomayor, Dr. Lydia Villa-Komaroff, Roberto Clemente, Cristela Alonzo, Cheech Marin, and others who continue to shape culture and break barriers.

He's also developing *Hija del Solara*, a supernatural Latina superhero saga deeply rooted in ancestral memory, myth, and generational strength. With Aztec and Mayan energy in its veins and San Jose attitude in its delivery, the series promises a bold, original universe where the fight is as internal as it is external. Expect high drama, higher stakes, and even a reimagined La Llorona that'll haunt your dreams—in the best way.

Sergio is also hard at work on *What Could Have Been* (coming 2026), a speculative deep dive into the lost futures of icons like Bruce and Brandon Lee, Tupac, Biggie, Aaliyah, and others who left us too soon. Equal parts heartbreaking and hopeful, the book imagines the art, change, and chaos they never got the chance to create.

But perhaps his most personal project is his latest: *10 CDs for a Penny: Growing Up Gen X with Bruises, Burnt Pop-Tarts, and Zero Therapy*—an unhinged, laugh-out-loud, sometimes gut-punching memoir-meets-cultural breakdown of what it meant to come of age when parenting was "figure it out," therapy was sarcasm, and dinner was whatever was in the microwave. It's his magnum opus to a generation that survived it all, with receipts, trauma, and pop culture references to prove it.

Sergio Serna lives in California, loves the Raiders like religion, and is always down for a good story, a bad decision, or both.

www.ingramcontent.com/pod-product-compliance
Lightning Source LLC
Chambersburg PA
CBHW050441150626
46551CB00028B/933